TAKE FIVE

MEDITATIONS WITH POPE BENEDICT XVI

D1598301

TAKE FIVE

MEDITATIONS WITH POPE BENEDICT XVI

MIKE AQUILINA & FR. KRIS D. STUBNA

Our Sunday Visitor Publishing Division
Our Sunday Visitor, Inc.
Huntington, Indiana 46750

Contents

Foreword

On October 6, 2008, the first working day of the 12th Synod of Bishops, dedicated to "The Word of God in the Life and Mission of the Church," Pope Benedict XVI spoke "off the cuff" to the assembled bishops and delegates and commented on Psalm 118, assigned for the Midday Office that morning. "All things serve you" was the verse that he targeted for his reflection. And he went right to the essentials, to the Word that gives birth to Creation: "All is created from the Word and all is called to serve the Word." He then marvelously unpacked the meaning of the Word in the history of salvation and in teaching, the Torah! He reached the highlight of his reflections by underlining the Word that became Flesh, the mystery of Christ the Word. When the Word became Flesh, Christ in effect said, "I am yours," to all creatures so that we can say with our whole being: "Lord, I am yours!"

Pope Benedict gets to the essentials. His thinking on our Catholic faith is always succinct. He has great clarity of mind. Simultaneously, he manifests a deep respect for the mystery of God, the mystery of faith, that is quite remarkable.

Last year, Father Kris Stubna and Mike Aquilina published a volume called *Take Five*, a book of meditations and practical spiritual guidance based on the writings of St. Ignatius of Loyola. Its success has prompted Our Sunday Visitor to publish a second volume of *Take Five*. This new book is based on the writings and teachings of our Holy Father, Pope Benedict XVI.

The book opens with a brief synopsis of the life of Pope Benedict. It is then divided into a number of topics of everyday spirituality. Each topic begins with an excerpt from one of the pope's writings. This is followed by a "Think About It" section outlining some points for thought or questions to be pondered, then by an imaginative re-creation of background for a verse or text from Holy Scripture. Finally, each topic has a "Remember" section and includes a practical "write-down line" to use all during the day. (These two men have to be teachers; they are fond of mnemonic devices!)

As a book of practical spirituality, this volume has every measure of success. The topics are useful, and the authors wisely let the pope have the greater word, while they act as coaches looking over our shoulders as we read, to offer a point for reflection and an always beautiful and relevant biblical text for prayer and reflection.

The final topic of the volume is the Rosary. The final words of the Remember section tell us to bring the prayers of the Rosary with us as a help to enter the silence of our hearts where God's Spirit dwells.

This little volume, pared to essentials, is just that. It is a guide to enter into silence with God, and there to discover God's Holy Spirit beckoning us to meet the Lord Jesus. Amen!

DANIEL CARDINAL DINARDO
Archbishop of Galveston-Houston

How to Use This Book

Most Christians spend a large part of their waking hours in activity related to their professional work. They put in long shifts — on the shop floor, in the classroom, in the office — and they spend additional time commuting to and from their labors. Thus, when they pass from this life, they will likely be judged to a great extent on what they did for a living.

Yet so many sermons and books on the spiritual life seem to ignore these everyday realities and focus instead on matters that are important — methods of meditation, volunteer work, almsgiving — but that hold a marginal place in the ordinary days of ordinary people.

In this book, we bring the rich teachings of Pope Benedict XVI to bear on the everyday circumstances of working life. Pope Benedict XVI has worked prodigiously through his life, and he has urged all the Church to do the same. He has written so many books and articles that his full bibliography can itself fill a book! And he produced these important works even as he held prestigious and responsible administrative and teaching positions.

He has been as busy a professional as you're likely to meet (or likely to become). Yet he has always been able to see the supernatural dimension of his tasks, even when they are mundane, difficult, or demanding of his entire attention.

How is he able to stay focused? He finds very practical ways to bring Christ into the workday, and he shares some of his methods with us through his books, sermons, letters, and his interviews. He writes about the dignity of work; about getting along with co-workers; about competitiveness; about the wise use of money and resources; and about the challenge of keeping your eye on the goal, which is not worldly success, but godly glory. These spiritual counsels make up the bulk of this book's meditations.

Even if we never reach the pope's level of prestige or proficiency, we can still achieve the (more important) spiritual goals that God has set for our work. This is what God wants; and God is all-powerful; so he will give us all we need to succeed.

The best way to learn from Pope Benedict is to get to know him first as a person and a teacher. Please begin by reading the story of his life, which is followed by a brief sketch of his spirituality.

The meditations may be read in any sequence that suits you. They do follow a certain logic, moving from elementary to ultimate matters. But you may find it occasionally useful to jump around in search of the subject that occupies your mind.

Each meditation begins with an excerpt from Pope Benedict's writings or teachings.

The meditation proceeds to a section titled **"Think About It."** There are a few points listed for you to consider in your prayer. You may refer them to yourself in God's presence, or refer them to God for answers, or both. Take time with each point. Don't rush. Wait quietly and patiently for God's response in your soul. He will not fail you — though his response may not be immediately sensible to you. Sometimes many years go by before we can see how God worked in our soul in prayer at a given moment.

Next is a section called **"Just Imagine."** A brief passage from Scripture is provided. Pope Benedict's prayer and doctrine flow from a vivid, prayerful experience of the Scriptures, especially the Gospels. Try to enter these biblical scenes as a participant or an onlooker so that you can personally experience the touch of Jesus, the teaching of Paul, and so on. Use your imagination!

Finally, you'll see a brief line or two with the heading **"Remember."** Copy this line onto a piece of paper and take it with you to work. Pull it out of your pocket occasionally and repeat it as a prayer. See if you can pray it from memory by the end of the day.

Try to build time into your schedule so that you can pray one meditation — or pray without these meditations — for at least twenty minutes per day, preferably in the morning. Our relationship with

God, like any personal relationship, grows deeper through conversation: intimate, heart-to-heart conversation. Workaholics look upon conversation as a luxury, but they're wrong. It is as necessary as drawing breath. It makes us human. And when our conversation is prayer, it makes us divine.

You wouldn't leave home without the tools of your trade. Try not to leave home without your morning prayer.

The Life of Pope Benedict XVI

He was born on Holy Saturday, April 16, 1927, and his parents baptized him Joseph Aloysius Ratzinger. The future pope described his childhood home as devout, his father as strict and deeply principled, and his mother as warm and kind. The Ratzinger family lived in the countryside. The children — Joseph and his brother and sister — were musically talented and often played together, with their parents joining in the singing.

"Religion was quite central"[1] to their family life. They prayed at every meal, attended daily Mass whenever possible, and eventually took up the practice of praying the Rosary together. Young Joseph had a great fondness for the liturgy, the Church's public worship. He received his first missal as a gift when he was in second grade, and he treasured it.

Throughout his childhood, Joseph's homeland was in turmoil. The treaty ending World War I had humiliated Germany, condemning it to long-term debt and economic ruin. The Nazi Party arose as a reaction, a reassertion of German identity. Adolf Hitler held the first Nazi meeting in Berlin just two weeks after Joseph's birth, and in the subsequent years gained a large following, especially in Bavaria, where the Ratzingers lived.

Joseph's father was a quiet but firm opponent of the Nazis. Even though he worked as a civil servant, he refused to join the party or its affiliated organizations. As a result, the family had to move several times. Hitler became chancellor in 1933 and established the Gestapo, his secret police. That same year, Pope Pius XI condemned the Nazi Party's eugenic policies. Nazi propaganda regularly sought to degrade Catholicism. In 1936, 150 Catholic youth leaders were arrested in Berlin. In the 1937 encyclical *Mit Brennender Sorge* ("With Burning Sorrow"), Pope Pius XI denounced Nazi racism and paganism. This further inflamed the Nazis' hostility toward the Church.

It was not easy to be a Catholic in this atmosphere. Young Joseph, like his father, resisted joining Nazi organizations; but enrollment in the Hitler Youth was routine at his school. He was given membership, but avoided attending activities. His teachers knew where he stood. Some respected him for his principles, and some even assisted him passively by looking the other way.

Despite the social upheavals and the household moves, the Ratzingers seem to have maintained a serene home. Joseph described a very gradual discernment of his priestly vocation. He entered minor seminary at age twelve in 1939. Seminarian status, however, did not exempt him from military service. With his classmates, he was drafted into the army antiaircraft corps in September 1943. They were released from service in 1944, only to be drafted again almost immediately. While guarding an automobile plant, young Joseph deserted his post and returned to his family home. With the Allies' victory, however, he was rounded up along with other members of the German military for debriefing and temporary internment. He stayed less than a month in a U.S.-run prisoner-of-war camp. Once released, he re-entered the seminary with his brother, Georg.

Both brothers were ordained on June 29, 1951. Joseph pursued doctoral studies and completed dissertations in 1953 and 1957, on St. Augustine and St. Bonaventure, respectively. At age thirty-two, he was already a full professor, teaching at the University of Bonn. He also bicycled to parishes nearby to preside at the sacraments — baptisms, burials, weddings, and confessions. Every Sunday he preached three homilies, two for adults and one for children. His children's homilies were so popular that they drew crowds of adults as well!

His life was busy. He advanced rapidly in his professional life. He served tirelessly in his pastoral life. Yet he never allowed his interior life to suffer. He remained faithful to the disciplines of prayer that he had learned as a child.

Joseph Ratzinger's career in the Church is well known. He served as a theological adviser to the influential Cardinal Joseph Frings at the Second Vatican Council. He published many books, establishing a reputation as a personally modest, but profound theologian. In 1977, Pope Paul VI ordained him archbishop of Munich-Freising and elevated him to the College of Cardinals.

In November 1981, Pope John Paul II summoned Archbishop Ratzinger to Rome to serve as prefect of the Congregation for the Doctrine of the Faith, the Vatican office that oversees orthodoxy in Catholic teaching. In that role, he became world famous — a face and a name recognizable by Catholics everywhere. He continued producing important works of theology, in spite of the heavy demands of his job.

On April 19, 2005, Cardinal Ratzinger was elected pope. He took the name Benedict XVI.[2]

The Spirit of Pope Benedict

In an interview in the year 2000, then-Cardinal Ratzinger described himself as "a perfectly ordinary Christian."[3] Though his positions in the Church — and his place in Church history — have certainly been extraordinary, "ordinary" may be the very best way to describe his spirituality. It's not ordinary because our parishes are brimful of brilliant and holy Catholics. It's ordinary, rather, because he has always emphasized the basics, the fundamentals, the traditional doctrines and devotions that are at the heart of the Catholic faith. He seems to have little personal interest in anything out of the ordinary — novelties, fads, trends, reports of apparitions, mystical phenomena, and so on. It's not that he rejects these things out of hand. It's just that he seems instinctively to choose the quiet way, the most modest way, the proven, well-worn way of everyday holiness.

What he said of his theology can be applied as well to his spirituality:

> I have never tried to create a system of my own, an individual theology. What is specific, if you want to call it that, is that I simply want to think in communion with the faith of the Church, and that means above all to think in communion with the great thinkers of the faith. The aim is not an isolated theology that I draw out of myself but one that opens as widely as possible into the common intellectual pathway of the faith. [4]

Those of us who live lives that aren't nearly so busy as his may wonder how he is able to cultivate a prayer life amid such a constant press of distractions and deadlines. Though an intensely private man, Pope Benedict has, on occasion, opened up to speak publicly about how he prays.

He said that he depends very much on daily routines — set prayers for set times. As soon as he wakes up, he recites a series of short traditional prayers, as a morning offering. After washing up, he goes to daily Mass, as he has since he was a child. At appointed times throughout the day, he also prays the official prayer of the Church — known as the Divine Office or the Liturgy of the Hours — which is a requirement for clergy and religious. Mass and the "Office": these he describes as "foundations of the day."[5] At noon, he says the Angelus. "And in between times, whenever I feel I need help, I can fit in a quick prayer."[6]

He sometimes compares prayer to a phone call, a two-way conversation that requires listening as well as talking:

> I know that he is always there. And he knows in any case who I am and what I am. Which is all the more reason for me to feel the need to call on him, to share my feelings with him, to talk with him. With him I can exchange views on the simplest and most intimate things, as well as on those that are weightiest and of great moment. It seems, somehow, normal for me to have occasion to talk to him all the time in everyday life.[7]

Listening is the harder part, because, as he explains, "God speaks quietly"[8]:

But he gives us all kinds of signs. In retrospect, especially, we can see that he has given us a little nudge through a friend, through a book, or through what we see as a failure — even through "accidents." Life is actually full of these silent indications. If I remain alert, then slowly they piece together a consistent whole, and I begin to feel how God is guiding me.[9]

Pope Benedict also recommends the Rosary, another form of prayer he has kept from his childhood: "I do it quite simply, just as my parents used to pray."[10] He tries to pray five mysteries a day, and he admits that concentration is a challenge for him: "I am too much of a restless spirit."[11] Sometimes he prays just one or two decades, as a break from work, "when I want to be quiet and to clear my head."[12]

He points out that the Rosary offers benefits in both the natural and supernatural orders. It calms the nerves even as it lifts up the soul. He goes on further to explain that

repetition is a part of prayer, of meditation, that repetition is a way of settling oneself into the rhythm of tranquility. It's not so much a matter of consciously concentrating on the meaning of each single word, but allowing myself on the contrary to be carried away by the calm of repetition and of steady rhythm. So much the more so, since this text does not lack content. It brings great images and visions and above all the figure of Mary — and then, through her, the figure of Jesus — before my eyes and in my soul.[13]

As pope, as cardinal, as bishop, or as priest, however, the man has never held up his own prayer life as a standard or a model. Instead, he has repeatedly emphasized the freedom that Catholic tradition presents to the individual believer: "Each of us can surely find something for ourselves out of the Church's treasury."[14] He counsels beginners to stop hesitating and just make a beginning: "Start by doing what believers do, even if it still makes no sense to you."[15] God will provide the light, the nurture, and the growth, all in due season.

And the pope should know. He has undergone dry spells in prayer, as everyone does: "Faith... needs the discipline of the dry periods; then something grows in the silence. Just as in the winter fields, despite appearances, the growth lies hidden."[16]

He recommends that we go to God, as a child goes to a kind father, and ask for the things we want and need. Yet "we know that what we ask is by no means always granted us.... 'Ask, and you will receive' certainly cannot mean that I can call God in as a handyman who will make my life easy every time I want something. Or who will take away suffering and questioning. On the contrary, it means that God definitely hears me and that what he grants me is, in the way known only to him, what is right for me."[17]

Though he is an extraordinary man, Pope Benedict has traveled a spiritual path that all of us can follow, even as we pursue quite ordinary lives, doing quite ordinary work. In his writing and preaching and speaking, he bids us to walk with him, taking small steps, day by day.

A Few Touchstones

If we pick up a book by Pope Benedict — or by Joseph Ratzinger — and we open to a random page, we will likely arrive very soon at the same judgment the *New York Times* made not long ago: "Benedict is one of the most intellectual men ever to serve as pope — and surely one of the most intellectual of current world leaders."[18] He is not always an easy read. Yet he does always strive to bring the discussion around to the basics of the faith. He has written profoundly in many fields of theology — including systematic, fundamental, biblical, historical, and liturgical, as well as Christology, eschatology, and ecclesiology — and many of his titles have become standard university textbooks in these fields. Yet he made his reputation with a book that bore the simple title *Introduction to Christianity*. He is able to push the limits of speculative discussion. But he is always seeking to shore up the foundations. He is among "the most intellectual" of intellectuals, but he is still the sensitive pastor whose children's homilies drew crowds to the parish churches in Bonn.

For this book of meditations, we have chosen only from his pastoral works written or delivered since his election as pope. They are addressed to the whole Church, the people in the parishes, who, like Benedict himself, are on a "personal search for 'the face of the Lord' (cf. Ps 27:8)."[19]

With us you may notice five "notes" he strikes often — five qualities that are representative of his spirituality. After all we've said so far, it should come as no surprise that they are common characteristics of the most basic Catholic piety. His approach to Christian living is:

1. **Christ-centered:** "Everything depends," the pope says, on "intimate friendship with Jesus." Jesus is faith's "point of reference."[20] "The disciple who walks with Jesus is thus caught up with him into communion with God. And that is what redemption means: this stepping beyond the limits of human nature."[21] Nowhere is this quality so evident as in his book *Jesus of Nazareth*.

2. **Biblical:** Pope Benedict XVI is a profound commentator on the Scriptures. He draws easily from both the Old and New Testa-

ments. For him, Scripture is at once "the measure that comes from God, the power directing the people," and also the book that "lives precisely within this people, even as this people transcends itself in the Scriptures."[22] His devotion to the Bible comes through strongly in scholarly studies such as *God's Word: Scripture, Tradition, Office*, but also in his collections of homilies, such as *What It Means to Be a Christian*.

3. **Liturgical:** To be a Christian is to worship, and the liturgy (especially the Mass) is the ritual public worship of the Church. A Christian should be "immersed in liturgy."[23] Liturgy brings out the poet in the pope, because liturgy "teaches [Christians] silence and singing again by opening to them the depths of the sea and teaching them to fly, the angels' mode of being." Liturgy "liberates us from ordinary, everyday activity and returns to us once more the depths and the heights, silence and song.... It sings with the angels. It is silent with the expectant depths of the universe. And that is how it redeems the earth."[24] See, for example, his book *The Spirit of the Liturgy*.

4. **Traditional:** Pope Benedict treats the communion of saints as his immediate family. He loves to tell the stories of the saints, and has

24

incorporated anecdotes from their lives even in his encyclicals. He invokes the ancient Church Fathers as if they are contemporaries. He considers the saints to be witnesses to the Sacred Tradition established once for all by the apostles and kept and guarded by the Catholic Church. Through his years as pope, he has composed several series of brief profiles of the saints, beginning with the apostles and continuing with the Fathers. He uses the incidents of their lives to bring out points of doctrine and Christian formation. (He is especially fond of St. Augustine.) This aspect of Pope Benedict's spirituality is best exemplified by his collections titled *The Fathers* and *The Apostles*.

5. **Marian:** Like many of his papal predecessors, Pope Benedict tends to end his preaching and even his extended pieces of writing with a Marian prayer or reflection. In an interview, he once described the Blessed Virgin as "an expression of the closeness of God." He added: "And the older I am, the more the Mother of God is important to me and close to me."[25] A "concrete human encounter with the Lord in his full reality" is, he says, "necessarily an encounter with his Mother, in whom the Israel of faith, the praying Church, has become a person.... One's relationship

with the Lord acquires its warmth and vitality only from this concrete proximity."[26]

He ends his 2007 encyclical letter *Spe Salvi* (on Christian hope) with a prayer to Mary:

You remain in the midst of the disciples as their Mother, as the Mother of hope. Holy Mary, Mother of God, our Mother, teach us to believe, to hope, to love with you. Show us the way to his Kingdom! Star of the Sea, shine upon us and guide us on our way! (n. 50)

And we, as we "take five," now begin to take his prayer as our own!

Notes

1. Joseph Cardinal Ratzinger, *Salt of the Earth: The Church at the End of the Millennium: An Interview with Peter Seewald* (San Francisco: Ignatius, 1997), p. 48.

2. For an excellent chronology of the life of Joseph Ratzinger — and an insightful account of his election to the papacy — see Matthew E. Bunson, D.Min., *We Have a Pope!: Benedict XVI* (Huntington, IN: Our Sunday Visitor, 2005).

3. *Salt of the Earth*, p. 54.

4. Ibid., p. 66.

5. Joseph Cardinal Ratzinger, *God and the World: A Conversation with Peter Seewald* (San Francisco: Ignatius, 2002), p. 19.

6. Ibid., p. 20.

7. Ibid., p. 18.

8. Ibid.

9. Ibid.

10. Ibid., p. 319.

11. Ibid., p. 320.

12. Ibid.

13. Ibid., p. 319.

14. Ibid., p. 20.

15. Ibid., p. 321.

16. Ibid.

17. Ibid., pp. 40-41.

18. Russell Shorto, "Keeping the Faith," *New York Times Magazine* (April 8, 2007).

19. Pope Benedict XVI, *Jesus of Nazareth* (New York: Doubleday, 2007), p. xxiii.

20. Ibid., p. xii.

21. Ibid., p. 8.

22. Ibid., p. xxi.

23. Joseph Cardinal Ratzinger, *A New Song for the Lord: Faith in Christ and Liturgy Today* (New York: Crossroad, 1997), p. 121.

24. Ibid., p. 127.

25. *God and the World*, p. 296.

26. Joseph Cardinal Ratzinger, *The Legacy of John Paul II: Images & Memories* (San Francisco: Ignatius, 2005), p. 22.

The Apostles. Huntington, IN: Our Sunday Visitor, 2007.

The Fathers. Huntington, IN: Our Sunday Visitor, 2008.

God's Word: Scripture, Tradition, Office. San Francisco: Ignatius, 2008.

God and the World: A Conversation with Peter Seewald. San Francisco: Ignatius, 2002.

Introduction to Christianity. San Francisco: Ignatius, 1990.

Jesus of Nazareth. New York: Doubleday, 2007.

The Legacy of John Paul II: Images & Memories. San Francisco: Ignatius, 2005.

A New Song for the Lord: Faith in Christ and Liturgy Today. New York: Crossroad, 1997.

Salt of the Earth: The Church at the End of the Millennium: An Interview with Peter Seewald. San Francisco: Ignatius, 1997.

The Spirit of the Liturgy. San Francisco: Ignatius, 2000.

What It Means to Be a Christian: Three Sermons. San Francisco: Ignatius, 2006.

1. The Value of Every Human Being

How many are the pilgrims you happen to meet throughout the year! I would like to ask you to see in each one of them the face of a brother or sister whom God sets on your path, a friendly albeit unknown person to be welcomed and helped with patient listening in the knowledge that we all belong to the one great human family. Is it not true... that we do not all live alongside one another purely by chance? Are we not all on the same journey as human beings and, hence, as brothers and sisters? For this reason, then, it is essential that each person strives to live his or her own life in an attitude of responsibility before God, recognizing him as the original source of his or her and everyone else's existence. Indeed, it is precisely by returning to this supreme Principle that one is enabled to perceive the unconditional value of every human being; it is thanks to this knowledge that the foundations for building a peaceful humanity can be laid. Let it be very clear: without the transcendent foundation which is God, society risks becoming a mere agglomeration of neighbors; it ceases to be a community of brothers and sisters, called to form one great family.

— *Address to Members of the Vatican's General Inspectorate for Public Security* (January 11, 2008)

- Everyone I meet is someone God has set on my path.
- No meetings are "chance" meetings.
- I should think of people as brothers and sisters, not merely neighbors.

"Are not five sparrows sold for two pennies? And not one of them is forgotten before God. Why, even the hairs of your head are all numbered. Fear not; you are of more value than many sparrows."

LUKE 12:6-7

Without God, society risks becoming a mere agglomeration of neighbors; it ceases to be a community of brothers and sisters.

2. Bringing Christ to Others

The more ardent the love for the Eucharist in the hearts of the Christian people, the more clearly will they recognize the goal of all mission: *to bring Christ to others*. Not just a theory or a way of life inspired by Christ, but the gift of his very person. Anyone who has not shared the truth of love with his brothers and sisters has not yet given enough.

— *Sacramentum Caritatis*, n. 86
(apostolic exhortation, February 22, 2007;
emphasis in original)

THINK ABOUT IT

- It is not enough to have Christ. I must bring him to others.
- At the heart of my religion is a person, not a theory or a catechism.
- Do my actions — even my speech and facial expressions — bear Christ to my co-workers?

JUST IMAGINE

Put on then, as God's chosen ones, holy and beloved, compassion, kindness, lowliness, meekness, and patience, forbearing one another and, if one has a complaint against another, forgiving each other; as the Lord has forgiven you, so you also must forgive.

And above all these put on love, which binds everything together in perfect harmony. And let the peace of Christ rule in your hearts, to which indeed you were called in the one body.

COLOSSIANS 3:12-15

REMEMBER

St. Francis of Assisi instructed his friars: Always preach the Gospel; use words only when you must. The example of a Christian life is the most powerful witness of all.

If you stay united with Christ, each one of you will be able to do great things. This is why, dear friends, you must not be afraid to dream with your eyes open of important projects of good and you must not let yourselves be discouraged by difficulties. Christ has confidence in you and wants you to be able to realize all your most noble and lofty dreams of genuine happiness. Nothing is impossible for those who trust in God and entrust themselves to him.

Look at the young Mary; the Angel proposed something truly inconceivable to her: participation, in the most involving way possible, in the greatest of God's plans, the salvation of humanity. Facing this proposal, Mary ... was distressed for she realized the smallness of her being before the omnipotence of God; and she asked herself: "How is it possible? Why should it be me?" Yet, ready to do the divine will, she promptly said her "yes," which changed her life and the history of all humanity....

I ask myself and I ask you: Can God's requests to us, however demanding they may seem, ever compare with what God asked the young Mary?... Since Mary truly knows what it means to respond generously to the Lord's requests, let us learn from her to say our own "yes."

— *Prayer Vigil with Young People,
Loreto, Italy* (September 1, 2007)

- Do I overcome my fear of failure and take on big projects?
- Do I allow myself to be discouraged by difficulties?
- Do I want to advance professionally for God's sake and not my own?
- Do I look to Mary as a mother, model, and teacher?

JUST IMAGINE

And the angel said to her,

> "The Holy Spirit will come upon you,
> and the power of the Most High will
>   overshadow you;
> therefore the child to be born will be called
>   holy,
> the Son of God....

For with God nothing will be impossible." And Mary said, "Behold, I am the handmaid of the Lord; let it be to me according to your word."

LUKE 1:35, 37-38

REMEMBER

I must not be afraid to dream with my eyes open of important projects.

4. The Longing of the Human Heart

St. Augustine, in the extended letter on prayer which he addressed to Proba, a wealthy Roman widow and mother of three consuls, once wrote this: ultimately we want only one thing — "the blessed life," the life which is simply life, simply "happiness." In the final analysis, there is nothing else that we ask for in prayer. Our journey has no other goal — it is about this alone. But then Augustine also says: looking more closely, we have no idea what we ultimately desire, what we would really like. We do not know this reality at all; even in those moments when we think we can reach out and touch it, it eludes us. "We do not know what we should pray for as we ought," he says, quoting St. Paul (Rom 8:26). All we know is that it is not this. Yet in not knowing, we know that this reality must exist. "There is therefore in us a certain learned ignorance (*docta ignorantia*), so to speak," he writes. We do not know what we would really like; we do not know this "true life"; and yet we know that there must be something we do not know towards which we feel driven.

— *Spe Salvi*, n. 11 (encyclical,
November 30, 2007)

- The desire for God is written in the human heart, because we were created by God and for God.
- Only when I rest in God will I find the truth, peace, and joy for which my heart never stops searching.
- In prayer, do I seek the truth and ask God for the courage to embrace his will, which is my only true happiness?

JUST IMAGINE

As a deer longs
  for flowing streams,
so longs my soul
  for you, O God.
My soul thirsts for God,
  for the living God.
When shall I come and behold
  the face of God?

PSALM 42:1-2

REMEMBER

God has placed the desire for happiness in the human heart in order to draw us to the One who alone can fulfill it (see *Catechism of the Catholic Church* [CCC] 1718).

Do not forget, however, that in order to carry out the mission entrusted to you, a proper technical and professional training is of course necessary; above all, though, you must ceaselessly cultivate within you a spirit of prayer and faithful adherence to the teachings of Christ and his Church. May the Virgin Mary, Star of the new evangelization, help and protect you always!

— *Address on the 75th Anniversary of the Founding of Vatican Radio* (March 3, 2006)

THINK ABOUT IT

- I should strive to know and do my work better, because I'm offering it to God.
- I should be ambitious in order to have a greater influence in my workplace or profession.
- Do I see my work — whatever it may be — as part of the new evangelization?

JUST IMAGINE

They were astonished beyond measure, saying, "He has done all things well."

MARK 7:37

To carry out the mission entrusted to me, a proper technical and professional training is necessary; above all, though, I must ceaselessly cultivate a spirit of prayer.

6. The Grandeur of the Worker

It came to my mind that in the New Testament, the word *tecton* appears, which was the profession of the Lord Jesus before his public ministry. We usually translate the word as "carpenter," because at that time houses were made mainly of wood. But more than a "carpenter," he was an "artisan" who must have been able to do all that was required in building a house.

Thus, in this sense, you are "colleagues" of Our Lord, who have done precisely what he would have willingly done, in accordance with what he had chosen, before proclaiming his great mission to the world. In this way the Lord desired to demonstrate the nobility of this craft.

In the Greek world, intellectual work alone was considered worthy of a free man. Manual work was left to slaves.

The biblical religion is quite different. Here, the Creator — who, according to a beautiful image, made man with his own hands — appears exactly as the example of a man who works with his hands, and in so doing works with his brain and his heart. Man imitates the Creator so that this world given to him by the Creator may be an inhabitable world.

This is apparent in the biblical narrative from the very start. But in the end, the nobility and grandeur of this work strongly emerges from the fact that Jesus was a *tecton*, an "artisan," a "worker."

— *Address to Those Who Renovated the Papal Apartments* (December 23, 2006)

THINK ABOUT IT

- Do I see Jesus as a colleague and go to him with my professional concerns?
- Am I aware that God is constantly at work through my labors?
- Do I view the work of others, no matter its pay or conditions, as noble and holy?

JUST IMAGINE

"Come to me, all who labor and are heavy laden, and I will give you rest."

MATTHEW 11:28

REMEMBER

I am a "colleague" of Our Lord, who has done precisely what he would have willingly done.

Today I would like to suggest another prayer intention, given the current news of numerous serious road accidents.... We must not resign ourselves to this sad reality! Human life is too precious a good, and death or incapacitation by causes which in most cases could have been avoided is most unworthy of man. A greater sense of responsibility is certainly essential, first and foremost on the part of drivers since accidents are often due to excessive speed or rash conduct. Driving a vehicle on public roads demands a moral and civic sense. To encourage the latter, the constant work of prevention, watchfulness, and penalization by the authorities in charge is indispensable. On the other hand, we as Church feel directly challenged on the ethical level: Christians must first of all make a personal examination of conscience regarding their own behavior as car drivers. Furthermore, may communities teach every man and woman to consider driving as another area in which to defend life and put love of neighbor into practice.

— *Angelus Address* (August 17, 2008)

THINK ABOUT IT

■ Do I put myself and others at risk by driving aggressively or carelessly?

- Am I distracted in my driving by talking on the phone or doing other things?
- Can I use the time spent traveling in the car for prayer, meditation, or spiritual conversation with my passengers — perhaps instead of talk radio?

They said to each other, "Did not our hearts burn within us while he talked to us on the road, while he opened to us the Scriptures?" And they rose that same hour and returned to Jerusalem; and they found the Eleven gathered together and those who were with them, who said, "The Lord has risen indeed, and has appeared to Simon!" Then they told what had happened on the road, and how he was known to them in the breaking of the bread.

LUKE 24:32-35

REMEMBER

Driving is a responsibility that requires patience, understanding, and tolerance of others.

8. What's My Style?

Jesus' style is unmistakable: it is the characteristic style of God who likes to do great things in a poor and humble manner. The solemnity of the accounts of the Covenant in the Book of Exodus leaves room in the Gospels for humble and discreet gestures which nevertheless contain an enormous potential for renewal. It is the logic of the Kingdom of God, not by chance represented by the tiny seed that becomes a great tree.

— *Homily at Port of Brindisi, Italy*
(June 15, 2008)

THINK ABOUT IT

- I should imitate God by doing small things with great care.
- I should not put off activities I find routine and boring.
- I should strive to accomplish helpful things, humbly and discreetly.

JUST IMAGINE

Another parable he put before them, saying, "The kingdom of heaven is like a grain of mustard seed which a man took and sowed in his field; it is the smallest of all seeds, but when it has grown it is the

greatest of shrubs and becomes a tree, so that the birds
of the air come and make nests in its branches."

MATTHEW 13:31-32

REMEMBER

It is the characteristic style of God who likes to do
great things in a poor and humble manner.

Our first duty, therefore, precisely in order to heal this world, is to be holy, configured to God; in this way we emanate a healing and transforming power that also acts on others, on history.... In this regard, it is useful to reflect that the Twelve Apostles were not perfect men, chosen for their moral and religious irreproachability. They were indeed believers, full of enthusiasm and zeal but at the same time marked by their human limitations, which were sometimes even serious. Therefore Jesus did not call them because they were already holy, complete, perfect, but so that they might become so, so that they might thereby also transform history, as it is for us, as it is for all Christians.

— *Homily at Port of Brindisi, Italy*
(June 15, 2008)

THINK ABOUT IT

- Is my own holiness my top priority?
- Do I deal patiently with the shortcomings of others, discreetly helping them to improve?
- God is working now to transform me and my co-workers, and thereby transform history.

Simon Peter ... fell down at Jesus' knees, saying, "Depart from me, for I am a sinful man, O Lord." For he was astonished, and all that were with him, at the catch of fish which they had taken.... And Jesus said to Simon, "Do not be afraid; henceforth you will be catching men." And when they had brought their boats to land, they left everything and followed him.

LUKE 5:8-11

REMEMBER

My first duty, precisely in order to heal this world, is to be holy.

10. Courage, Daring

Dare to dedicate your life to courageous choices, not alone of course, but with the Lord! Give this city the impetus and enthusiasm that flow from your living experience of faith, an experience that does not spoil the expectations of human life but exalts them by participation in the very experience of Christ.... My hope for all is that faith in the Triune God will imbue in every person and in every community the fervor of love and hope, the joy of loving one another as brothers and sisters and of putting oneself humbly at the service of others. This is the "leaven" that causes humanity to grow, the light that shines in the world.

— *Homily in Savona, Italy* (May 17, 2008)

THINK ABOUT IT

- Do I include God in my decision-making process?
- Do I consistently choose courageously and "with the Lord"?
- Do I give a positive witness in the midst of my city?

"The kingdom of heaven is like leaven which a woman took and hid in three measures of meal, till it was all leavened."

MATTHEW 13:33

REMEMBER

I will dare to dedicate my life to courageous choices.

11. Signs of the Kingdom

Praying fervently for the coming of the Kingdom also means being constantly alert for the signs of its presence, and working for its growth in every sector of society. It means facing the challenges of present and future with confidence in Christ's victory and a commitment to extending his reign. It means not losing heart in the face of resistance, adversity, and scandal. It means overcoming every separation between faith and life, and countering false gospels of freedom and happiness. It also means rejecting a false dichotomy between faith and political life, since, as the Second Vatican Council put it, "there is no human activity — even in secular affairs — which can be withdrawn from God's dominion" (*Lumen Gentium*, n. 36). It means working to enrich ... society and culture with the beauty and truth of the Gospel, and never losing sight of that great hope which gives meaning and value to all the other hopes which inspire our lives.

— *Homily During Mass at Yankee Stadium*
(April 20, 2008)

THINK ABOUT IT

■ I should face all challenges with confidence that Christ will win.

- I should go immediately to God when faced with trouble or scandal.
- Do I see all activity — work, leisure, family life — as an offering to God?

So, whether you eat or drink, or whatever you do, do all to the glory of God. Give no offense to Jews or to Greeks or to the Church of God, just as I try to please all men in everything I do, not seeking my own advantage, but that of many, that they may be saved.

1 Corinthians 10:31-33

Praying for the coming of the Kingdom also means working for its growth, always confident in Christ's victory.

12. Your Witness at Work

And what of today? Who bears witness to the Good News of Jesus on the streets of New York, in the troubled neighborhoods of large cities, in the places where the young gather, seeking someone in whom they can trust? God is our origin and our destination, and Jesus the way. The path of that journey twists and turns — just as it did for our saints — through the joys and the trials of ordinary, everyday life: within your families, at school or college, during your recreation activities, and in your parish communities. All these places are marked by the culture in which you are growing up. As young Americans you are offered many opportunities for personal development, and you are brought up with a sense of generosity, service, and fairness. Yet you do not need me to tell you that there are also difficulties: activities and mind-sets which stifle hope, pathways which seem to lead to happiness and fulfillment but in fact end only in confusion and fear.

— *Address to Young People and Seminarians, New York* (April 19, 2008)

THINK ABOUT IT

- If I do not stand up for Christ, who will?
- What are the things that stifle my friends' hope and lead them to confusion?

■ I must keep focused on the goal: God is my origin and destination.

"Enter by the narrow gate; for the gate is wide and the way is easy, that leads to destruction, and those who enter by it are many. For the gate is narrow and the way is hard, that leads to life, and those who find it are few."

MATTHEW 7:13-14

REMEMBER

God is our origin and our destination, and Jesus the way.

Put simply, we are no longer able to hear God — there are too many different frequencies filling our ears. What is said about God strikes us as pre-scientific, no longer suited to our age. Along with the hardness of hearing or outright deafness, where God is concerned, we naturally lose our ability to speak with him and to him. And so we end up losing a decisive capacity for perception. We risk losing our inner senses. This weakening of our capacity for perception drastically and dangerously curtails the range of our relationship with reality in general. The horizon of our life is disturbingly foreshortened. The Gospel tells us that Jesus put his fingers in the ears of the deaf-mute, touched the sick man's tongue with spittle, and said, "*Ephphata* — be opened." The Evangelist has preserved for us the original Aramaic word which Jesus spoke, and thus he brings us back to that very moment. What happened then was unique, but it does not belong to a distant past. Jesus continues to do the same things anew, even today. At our baptism he touched each of us and said, "*Ephphata* — be opened," thus enabling us to hear God's voice and to be able to talk to him.

> — *Homily During Mass,*
> *Munich, Germany*
> (September 10, 2006)

- God speaks to us through his saving Word.
- Obedience to God's Word requires me to make time to listen to his voice.
- Am I like Mary, who hears God's Word and responds with trust: "Let it be [done] to me according to your word" (Lk 1:38)?

JUST IMAGINE

"'For this people's heart has grown dull,
    and their ears are heavy of hearing,
    and their eyes they have closed,
lest they should perceive with their eyes,
    and hear with their ears,
and understand with their heart,
    and turn for me to heal them.'

But blessed are your eyes, for they see, and your ears, for they hear. Truly, I say to you, many prophets and righteous men longed to see what you see, and did not see it, and to hear what you hear, and did not hear it."

MATTHEW 13:15-17

REMEMBER

The prophet Elijah learned that God's voice was not in earthquake, lightning, wind, or fire. God's voice often comes as a quiet whisper in the silence of my heart.

14. Choosing Truth

Have you noticed how often the call for freedom is made without ever referring to the truth of the human person? Some today argue that respect for freedom of the individual makes it wrong to seek truth, including the truth about what is good. In some circles to speak of truth is seen as controversial or divisive, and consequently best kept in the private sphere. And in truth's place — or better said its absence — an idea has spread which, in giving value to everything indiscriminately, claims to assure freedom and to liberate conscience. This we call relativism. But what purpose has a "freedom" which, in disregarding truth, pursues what is false or wrong? How many young people have been offered a hand which in the name of freedom or experience has led them to addiction, to moral or intellectual confusion, to hurt, to a loss of self-respect, even to despair and so tragically and sadly to the taking of their own life? Dear friends, truth is not an imposition. Nor is it simply a set of rules. It is a discovery of the One who never fails us; the One whom we can always trust. In seeking truth we come to live by belief because ultimately truth is a person: Jesus Christ. That is why authentic freedom is not an opting out. It is an opting in; nothing less than letting go of self

55

and allowing oneself to be drawn into Christ's very being for others (cf. *Spe Salvi*, n. 28).

— *Address to Young People and Seminarians,*
New York (April 19, 2008)

THINK ABOUT IT

- Truth is liberating. A traveler with a map is freer than a traveler without one.
- I lose nothing by choosing the truth. All is gain.
- Sin is a path not to freedom, but enslavement.

JUST IMAGINE

Jesus said . . . , "I am the way, and the truth, and the life; no one comes to the Father, but by me."

JOHN 14:6

REMEMBER

Truth is not simply a set of rules. It is ultimately a person: Jesus Christ.

There used to be a form of devotion — perhaps less practiced today but quite widespread not long ago — that included the idea of "offering up" the minor daily hardships that continually strike at us like irritating "jabs," thereby giving them a meaning. Of course, there were some exaggerations and perhaps unhealthy applications of this devotion, but we need to ask ourselves whether there may not after all have been something essential and helpful contained within it. What does it mean to offer something up? Those who did so were convinced that they could insert these little annoyances into Christ's great "com-passion" so that they somehow became part of the treasury of compassion so greatly needed by the human race. In this way, even the small inconveniences of daily life could acquire meaning and contribute to the economy of good and of human love. Maybe we should consider whether it might be judicious to revive this practice ourselves.

— *Spe Salvi*, n. 40
(encyclical, November 30, 2007)

THINK ABOUT IT

- I should "offer up" inconveniences and pains instead of complaining about them.

- I should recognize that no suffering is valueless. Think of the Cross.
- I unite my troubles with Jesus on the Cross.

Now I rejoice in my sufferings for your sake, and in my flesh I complete what is lacking in Christ's afflictions for the sake of his body, that is, the Church.

COLOSSIANS 1:24

Even the small inconveniences of daily life can acquire meaning and contribute to the economy of good and of human love.

Day by day, man experiences many greater or lesser hopes, different in kind according to the different periods of his life. Sometimes one of these hopes may appear to be totally satisfying without any need for other hopes. Young people can have the hope of a great and fully satisfying love; the hope of a certain position in their profession, or of some success that will prove decisive for the rest of their lives. When these hopes are fulfilled, however, it becomes clear that they were not, in reality, the whole. It becomes evident that man has need of a hope that goes further. It becomes clear that only something infinite will suffice for him, something that will always be more than he can ever attain.

— *Spe Salvi*, n. 30
(encyclical, November 30, 2007)

THINK ABOUT IT

- Hope is God's gift, not something I can achieve by my own strength.
- Do I aim for limited hopes that are bound to disappoint me?
- Do I demand from others a satisfaction that only God can give?

I consider that the sufferings of this present time are not worth comparing with the glory that is to be revealed to us. For the creation waits with eager longing for the revealing of the sons of God; for the creation was subjected to futility, not of its own will but by the will of him who subjected it in hope; because the creation itself will be set free from its bondage to decay and obtain the glorious liberty of the children of God. We know that the whole creation has been groaning with labor pains together until now; and not only the creation, but we ourselves, who have the first fruits of the Spirit, groan inwardly as we wait for adoption as sons, the redemption of our bodies. For in this hope we were saved. Now hope that is seen is not hope. For who hopes for what he sees? But if we hope for what we do not see, we wait for it with patience.

ROMANS 8:18-25

REMEMBER

When our earthly hopes are fulfilled, it becomes clear that only something infinite will suffice.

When no one listens to me anymore, God still listens to me. When I can no longer talk to anyone or call upon anyone, I can always talk to God. When there is no longer anyone to help me deal with a need or expectation that goes beyond the human capacity for hope, he can help me. When I have been plunged into complete solitude...; if I pray I am never totally alone.

— *Spe Salvi*, n. 32
(encyclical, November 30, 2007)

THINK ABOUT IT

- I must make an effort to go to God first, considering my needs in prayer.
- I should not expect people to do what only God can do for me. It is unfair to them and to God.
- When I feel alone, do I acknowledge that God is with me?

JUST IMAGINE

"The hour is coming, indeed it has come, when you will be scattered, every man to his home, and will leave me alone; yet I am not alone, for the Father is with me."

JOHN 16:32

REMEMBER

When no one listens to me anymore, God still listens to me.

When we pray properly we undergo a process of inner purification which opens us up to God and thus to our fellow human beings as well. In prayer we must learn what we can truly ask of God — what is worthy of God. We must learn that we cannot pray against others. We must learn that we cannot ask for the superficial and comfortable things that we desire at this moment — that meager, misplaced hope that leads us away from God. We must learn to purify our desires and our hopes.

— *Spe Salvi*, n. 33
(encyclical, November 30, 2007)

THINK ABOUT IT

- Do I expect prayer to change God's mind — or mine?
- Is my prayer life reshaping my hopes?
- Do I want to want the right things?

JUST IMAGINE

"You have heard that it was said, 'You shall love your neighbor and hate your enemy.' But I say to you, Love your enemies and pray for those who persecute you."

MATTHEW 5:43-44

In prayer I must learn what I can truly ask of God —
what is worthy of God.

We must free ourselves from the hidden lies with which we deceive ourselves. God sees through them, and when we come before God, we too are forced to recognize them. "But who can discern his errors? Clear me from hidden faults," prays the Psalmist (Ps 19:12). Failure to recognize my guilt, the illusion of my innocence, does not justify me and does not save me, because I am culpable for the numbness of my conscience and my incapacity to recognize the evil in me for what it is. If God does not exist, perhaps I have to seek refuge in these lies, because there is no one who can forgive me; no one who is the true criterion. Yet my encounter with God awakens my conscience in such a way that it no longer aims at self-justification, and is no longer a mere reflection of me and those of my contemporaries who shape my thinking, but it becomes a capacity for listening to the Good itself.

— *Spe Salvi*, n. 33
(encyclical, November 30, 2007)

THINK ABOUT IT

■ I must be honest about myself in God's presence.

■ I must resolve to be regular about examining my conscience and confessing my sins.

■ I want to know the truth about myself.

"Two men went up into the temple to pray, one a Pharisee and the other a tax collector. The Pharisee stood and prayed thus with himself, 'God, I thank you that I am not like other men, extortioners, unjust, adulterers, or even like this tax collector. I fast twice a week, I give tithes of all that I get.' But the tax collector, standing far off, would not even lift up his eyes to heaven, but beat his breast, saying, 'God, be merciful to me a sinner!' I tell you, this man went down to his house justified rather than the other; for every one who exalts himself will be humbled, but he who humbles himself will be exalted."

LUKE 18:10-14

I must free myself from the hidden lies with which I deceive myself.

For prayer to develop this power of purification, it must on the one hand be something very personal, an encounter between my intimate self and God, the living God. On the other hand it must be constantly guided and enlightened by the great prayers of the Church and of the saints, by liturgical prayer, in which the Lord teaches us again and again how to pray properly. Cardinal Nguyen Van Thuan, in his book of spiritual exercises, tells us that during his life there were long periods when he was unable to pray and that he would hold fast to the texts of the Church's prayer: the Our Father, the Hail Mary, and the prayers of the liturgy (*Testimony of Hope*, pp. 121ff). Praying must always involve this intermingling of public and personal prayer. This is how we can speak to God and how God speaks to us.

— *Spe Salvi*, n. 34
(encyclical, November 30, 2007)

THINK ABOUT IT

- What do I do when I find myself unable to pray?
- Do I know and use the great prayers of the Church's tradition?
- How can I improve my public prayer? How can I improve my personal prayer?

"Pray then like this:

> Our Father who art in heaven,
> Hallowed be thy name.
> Thy kingdom come.
> Thy will be done,
>> On earth as it is in heaven.
> Give us this day our daily bread;
> And forgive us our trespasses,
>> As we forgive those who trespass against
>> us;
> And lead us not into temptation,
> But deliver us from evil."

MATTHEW 6:9-13

REMEMBER

In public and in personal prayer, I speak to God and God speaks to me.

Certainly we must do whatever we can to reduce suffering: to avoid as far as possible the suffering of the innocent; to soothe pain; to give assistance in overcoming mental suffering.... Indeed, we must do all we can to overcome suffering, but to banish it from the world altogether is not in our power. This is simply because we are unable to shake off our finitude and because none of us is capable of eliminating the power of evil, of sin which, as we plainly see, is a constant source of suffering. Only God is able to do this: only a God who personally enters history by making himself man and suffering within history. We know that this God exists, and hence that this power to "take away the sin of the world" (Jn 1:29) is present in the world. Through faith in the existence of this power, hope for the world's healing has emerged in history. It is, however, hope — not yet fulfillment; hope that gives us the courage to place ourselves on the side of good even in seemingly hopeless situations, aware that, as far as the external course of history is concerned, the power of sin will continue to be a terrible presence....

We can try to limit suffering, to fight against it, but we cannot eliminate it. It is when we attempt to avoid suffering by withdrawing from anything that might involve hurt, when we try to spare ourselves the effort and pain of pursuing truth, love, and goodness, that we drift into a life of emptiness, in which there may be almost no pain, but the dark sensation of meaninglessness and abandonment is all the greater. It is not by sidestepping or fleeing from suffering that we are healed, but rather by our capacity for accepting it, maturing through it and finding meaning through union with Christ, who suffered with infinite love.

— *Spe Salvi*, n. 36-37
(encyclical, November 30, 2007)

THINK ABOUT IT

- I must keep in mind that it is God who saves people, even as I do what I can to ease their pain.
- Do I allow suffering to limit my compassion or my quest for truth?
- Have I experienced good things emerging from suffering that may not have been possible otherwise?

JUST IMAGINE

And he called to him the multitude with his disciples, and said to them, "If any man would come after me, let him deny himself and take up his cross and follow me"

MARK 8:34

It is not by fleeing from suffering that I am healed, but rather by my capacity for maturing through it.

22. Confess Regularly

It is very helpful to confess with a certain regularity. It is true: our sins are always the same, but we clean our homes, our rooms, at least once a week, even if the dirt is always the same; in order to live in cleanliness, in order to start again. Otherwise, the dirt might not be seen but it builds up. Something similar can be said about the soul, for me myself: if I never go to confession, my soul is neglected and in the end I am always pleased with myself and no longer understand that I must always work hard to improve, that I must make progress. And this cleansing of the soul which Jesus gives us in the Sacrament of Confession helps us to make our consciences more alert, more open, and hence, it also helps us to mature spiritually and as human persons.

— *Catechetical Meeting with Children*
Who Had Received Their First Communion
(October 15, 2005)

THINK ABOUT IT

- Do I go to confession regularly? Do I go often enough?
- I will make an effort to prepare very well for my next confession.
- How does the practice of confession form my conscience?

Jesus began to preach, saying, "Repent, for the kingdom of heaven is at hand."

MATTHEW 4:17

If I never go to confession, my soul is neglected and in the end I am always pleased with myself and no longer understand that I must make progress.

Man ... has the duty to make all the earth's goods fruitful, committing himself to use them to satisfy the multiple needs of each member of the human family.... With the heart of a faithful administrator man must, therefore, administer the resources entrusted to him by God, putting them at the disposition of all. In other words, one must avoid that the profit accrue only to the individual or that forms of collectivism oppress personal freedom. Economic or commercial interests must never become exclusive, because, indeed, this would be to mortify human dignity. Since the process of globalization ... invests ever more in the field of culture, economics, finance, and politics, the great challenge today is "to globalize" not only economic and commercial interests, but also the expectations of solidarity.... [E]conomic growth must never be separate from seeking integral human and social development.

— *Address to Members of Centesimus Annus-Pro Pontifice Foundation* (May 31, 2008)

THINK ABOUT IT

- Do I consider the social consequences of my purchases and investments?
- Does my work involve the exploitation of others? If so, how can I change that?

- Over what part of creation has God made me a steward?

JUST IMAGINE

And Jesus said to his disciples, "Truly, I say to you, it will be hard for a rich man to enter the kingdom of heaven. Again I tell you, it is easier for a camel to go through the eye of a needle than for a rich man to enter the kingdom of God."

MATTHEW 19:23-24

REMEMBER

The great challenge today is "to globalize" not only economic and commercial interests, but also the expectations of solidarity.

24. Effective Communications

The diverse forms of communication — dialogue, prayer, teaching, witness, proclamation — and their different instruments — the press, electronics, the visual arts, music, voice, gestural art and contact — are all manifestations of the fundamental nature of the human person. It is communication that reveals the person, that creates authentic and community relationships, and which permits human beings to mature in knowledge, wisdom, and love. However, communication is not the simple product of a pure and fortuitous chance or of our human capacity. In the light of the biblical message, it reflects, rather, our participation in the creative, communicative, and unifying Trinitarian Love which is the Father, the Son, and the Holy Spirit. God has created us to be united to him and he has given us the gift and the duty of communication, because he wants us to obtain this union, not alone, but through our knowledge, our love, and our service to him and to our brothers and sisters in a communicative and loving relationship.

— *Address to Convention Organized by the Pontifical Council for Social Communications* (May 23, 2008)

- I must be aware that all my communications reflect my share in God's nature.
- Do I take care to write and speak clearly, as an act of charity toward others?
- Do I always write and speak the truth?

"Let what you say be simply 'Yes' or 'No'; anything more than this comes from the Evil One."

MATTHEW 5:37

God has given me the gift of communication because he wants me to obtain union with him, not alone, but through my service to him and to others.

There are times ... when we might be tempted to seek a certain fulfillment apart from God. Jesus himself asked the Twelve: "Do you also wish to go away?" Such drifting away perhaps offers the illusion of freedom. But where does it lead? To whom would we go? For in our hearts we know that it is the Lord who has "the words of eternal life" (Jn 6:67-68). To turn away from him is only a futile attempt to escape from ourselves. God is with us in the reality of life, not the fantasy! It is embrace, not escape, that we seek! So the Holy Spirit gently but surely steers us back to what is real, what is lasting, what is true. It is the Spirit who leads us back into the communion of the Blessed Trinity!

— *World Youth Day Vigil*
(July 19, 2008)

THINK ABOUT IT

- What things tempt me most strongly away from God?
- What do I fear about God? What do I wish to escape?
- Do I realize that there is no lasting happiness apart from God, and that lesser "fulfillments" can bring greater misery?

"No one is good but God alone."

MARK 10:18

God is with me in the reality of life, not the fantasy!
It is embrace, not escape, that I seek!

26. End Times Begin Now

We have been told with regard to Christ's definitive return in the *parousia* that he will not come alone but with all his saints. Thus, every saint who enters history already constitutes a tiny portion of Christ's Second Coming, his new entry into time which shows us his image in a new dimension and assures us of his presence. Jesus Christ does not belong to the past, nor is he confined to a distant future whose coming we do not even have the courage to seek. He arrives with a great procession of saints. Together with his saints he is already on his way towards us, towards our present.

— *Christmas Address to Members of the Curia*
(December 21, 2007)

THINK ABOUT IT

- I should have no anxiety about the future, or even the end of history.
- I should look with hope and longing toward the day I may join with the saints.
- Christ is on his way toward us — toward me!

JUST IMAGINE

He who testifies to these things says, "Surely I am coming soon." Amen. Come, Lord Jesus!

REVELATION 22:20

Jesus Christ does not belong to the past, nor is he confined to a distant future. He is already on his way toward our present.

May you always walk joyfully on the road of life with Jesus. One day he said: "I am the way" (Jn 14: 6). Jesus is the way that leads to true life, life that never ends. It is often a narrow, uphill road, but if we let ourselves be attracted by him it is always marvelous, like a steep mountain path: the more steeply it rises, the better one can admire from on high new views even more beautiful and extensive. There is the effort of walking, but we are not alone: we help each other, we wait for one another, we lend a hand to those who have been left behind.... The important thing is not to get lost, not to stray from the path, otherwise we risk ending in a ravine, of getting lost in the woods!

— *Address to Children of Italian Catholic Action*
(December 20, 2007)

THINK ABOUT IT

- I should take care that none of my companions strays from the path or gets left behind.
- I should cultivate an appreciation for the path along which God has led me. It is distinctively mine.
- I must make an effort to walk joyfully, even when the path goes steeply uphill.

Jesus said to him, "I am the way, and the truth, and the life; no one comes to the Father, but by me."

JOHN 14:6

If I let myself be attracted by him, the way is always marvelous, like a steep mountain path.

28. The Power of Beauty

John Paul II ... recounted that after the war he was visited by a Russian official who was a scientist and who said to him as a scientist: "I am certain that God does not exist. Yet, if I am in the mountains, surrounded by his majestic beauty, by his grandeur, I am equally sure that the Creator does exist and that God exists."

The beauty of creation is one of the sources where we can truly touch God's beauty, we can see that the Creator exists and is good, which is true as Sacred Scripture says in the Creation Narrative, that is, that God conceived of this world and made it with his heart, his will, and his reason, and he found it good.

We too must be good in order to have an open heart and to perceive God's true presence.

Then, hearing the Word of God in the solemn liturgical celebrations, in celebrations of faith, in the great music of faith, we feel this presence. I remember at this moment another little story which a bishop on his *ad limina* visit told me a little while ago.

There was a very intelligent woman who was not a Christian. She began to listen to the great music of Bach, Handel, and Mozart. She was fascinated and said one day, "I must find the source of this beauty," and the woman converted to Christianity, to the

Catholic faith, because she had discovered that this beauty has a source, and the source is the presence of Christ in hearts, it is the revelation of Christ in this world.

— Prayer Vigil with Young People, Loreto, Italy (September 1, 2007)

- Do I strive to appreciate what is beautiful in nature and culture? Do I see it as a reflection of God's order and power?
- Do I appreciate the beauties of the liturgy?
- Do I appreciate how beauty can attract people to the faith?

JUST IMAGINE

For what can be known about God is plain to them, because God has shown it to them. Ever since the creation of the world his invisible nature, namely, his eternal power and deity, has been clearly perceived in the things that have been made.

ROMANS 1:19-20

REMEMBER

The beauty of creation is one of the sources where I can truly touch God's beauty.

You are on the verge of deciding on your future. Are you doing so in the light of Christ, asking him, "What do you want of me?" Are you following the path he points out to you with generosity and confidence, knowing that as baptized people we are all, without exception, called to holiness and to be living members of the Church on whatever path we take in life?

— *Address to Young People in the*
"Youth Mission" of Madrid (August 9, 2007)

THINK ABOUT IT

- I should consider my future in God's presence, knowing that he has a plan for me.
- I should ask for light so that I can understand his plan and my vocation.
- I should thank him for calling me to be a saint.

JUST IMAGINE

As they were going along the road, a man said to him, "I will follow you wherever you go." And Jesus said to him, "Foxes have holes, and birds of the air have nests; but the Son of man has nowhere to lay his head." ... Another said, "I will follow you, Lord; but let me first say farewell to those at my home."

Jesus said to him, "No one who puts his hand to the plow and looks back is fit for the kingdom of God."

LUKE 9:57-58, 61-62

REMEMBER

We are all, without exception, called to holiness on whatever path we take in life.

30. Loving God and Neighbor

Being in communion with Jesus Christ draws us into his "being for all"; it makes it our own way of being. He commits us to live for others, but only through communion with him does it become possible truly to be there for others, for the whole. In this regard I would like to quote the great Greek Doctor of the Church, Maximus the Confessor, who begins by exhorting us to prefer nothing to the knowledge and love of God, but then quickly moves on to practicalities: "The one who loves God cannot hold on to money but rather gives it out in God's fashion... in the same manner in accordance with the measure of justice." Love of God leads to participation in the justice and generosity of God towards others. Loving God requires an interior freedom from all possessions and all material goods: the love of God is revealed in responsibility for others.

— *Spe Salvi*, n. 28
(encyclical, November 30, 2007)

THINK ABOUT IT

- Do I build my love for others upon the foundation of my love for God?
- Am I distracted from God by the temptations of status, money, and other things?

■ Do I see the face of God in others who come my way? Do I serve them, then, in love?

"Teacher, what good deed must I do, to have eternal life?" And he said to him, "Why do you ask me about what is good? One there is who is good. If you would enter life, keep the commandments." He said to him, "Which?" And Jesus said, "You shall not kill, You shall not commit adultery, You shall not steal, You shall not bear false witness, Honor your father and mother, and, You shall love your neighbor as yourself." The young man said to him, "All these I have observed; what do I still lack?" Jesus said to him, "If you would be perfect, go, sell what you possess and give to the poor, and you will have treasure in heaven; and come, follow me." When the young man heard this he went away sorrowful; for he had great possessions.

MATTHEW 19:16-22

REMEMBER

The whole of the law and all the prophets can be summed up in the greatest of all the commandments: to love God and neighbor.

In praising you for your commitment, I urge you always to view your work as a true mission to be carried out with passion and patience, kindness, and a spirit of faith. Always be concerned to present a welcoming image..., aware that the Gospel message also passes through your consistent Christian testimony.

— *Visit to the Vatican Apostolic Library*
(June 25, 2007)

THINK ABOUT IT

- Do I view my work as a mission, a field for apostolic witness?
- The things I do — for better or for worse — define for others the actions of a Christian.
- Do I work with passion and patience?

JUST IMAGINE

"Let your light so shine before men, that they may see your good works and give glory to your Father who is in heaven."

MATTHEW 5:16

REMEMBER

The Gospel message also passes through my consistent Christian testimony.

This proper way of serving others also leads to humility. The one who serves does not consider himself superior to the one served, however miserable his situation at the moment may be. Christ took the lowest place in the world — the Cross — and by this radical humility he redeemed us and constantly comes to our aid. Those who are in a position to help others will realize that in doing so they themselves receive help; being able to help others is no merit or achievement of their own. This duty is a grace. The more we do for others, the more we understand and can appropriate the words of Christ: "We are useless servants" (Lk 17:10). We recognize that we are not acting on the basis of any superiority or greater personal efficiency, but because the Lord has graciously enabled us to do so.

— *Deus Caritas Est*, n. 35
(encyclical, December 25, 2005)

THINK ABOUT IT

- Where my treasure is, there also will my heart be (see Mt 6:21).
- "Blessed are the poor in spirit, for theirs is the kingdom of heaven" (Mt 5:3).

■ Humility reminds me that I am totally dependent on God and his grace; all that I have is a gift.

[Jesus] rose from supper, laid aside his garments, and tied a towel around himself. Then he poured water into a basin, and began to wash the disciples' feet, and to wipe them with the towel that was tied around him.... When he had washed their feet, and taken his garments, and resumed his place, he said to them, "Do you know what I have done to you?... I have given you an example, that you also should do as I have done to you."

JOHN 13:4-5, 12, 15

It is only by the grace of God that I am able to achieve the potential for which I have been created, and it is by the grace of God that I will be saved.

Every gesture of genuine love, even the smallest, contains within it a spark of the infinite mystery of God: the attentive concern for a brother, drawing near to him, sharing his need, caring for his wounds, taking responsibility for his future, everything to the last detail becomes "theological" when it is animated by the Spirit of Christ.

— *Marian Vigil, Vatican Gardens* (May 31, 2007)

THINK ABOUT IT

- I should find many opportunities for kindness in an ordinary day.
- It costs me nothing to smile for others and show concern for the things that are important to them.
- I should strive to remember the names and interests of people I meet.

JUST IMAGINE

"His master said to him, 'Well done, good and faithful servant; you have been faithful over a little, I will set you over much; enter into the joy of your master.'"

MATTHEW 25:21

Every gesture of genuine love, even the smallest, contains within it a spark of the infinite mystery of God.

All this, dear friends, is part of your daily labor, of a task that must not be carried out in an abstract or purely intellectual way, but with attention to the thousands of aspects of the practical life of a people, its problems, its needs, and its hopes.

May the certainty that the Christian faith is open to "whatever is true, honorable, just, pure, lovely, gracious" in the culture of peoples, as the Apostle Paul taught the Philippians (cf. 4:8), sustain you and give you courage in your labors.

Thus, continue in your work with this spirit and this attitude, bearing a shining witness of a profoundly Christian life and consequently remaining tenaciously united to Christ, so that you can look at the world with his own eyes.

— *Address to the Media of the Italian Bishops' Conference* (June 2, 2006)

THINK ABOUT IT

■ Do I recognize that work can be a holy offering to God?

■ Do I see my work as taking part in God's creation?

■ Do I stay close to Christ in my thoughts throughout the workday?

As he landed he saw a great throng, and he had compassion on them, because they were like sheep without a shepherd; and he began to teach them many things.

MARK 6:34

I should remain tenaciously united to Christ, so that I can look at the world with his own eyes.

35. A Word About the Word

One must not read Sacred Scripture as one reads any kind of historical book, such as, for example, Homer, Ovid, or Horace; it is necessary truly to read it as the Word of God, that is, entering into a conversation with God.

One must start by praying and talking to the Lord: "Open the door to me." And what St. Augustine often says in his homilies, "I knocked at the door of the Word to find out at last what the Lord wants to say to me," seems to me to be a very important point. One should not read Scripture in an academic way, but with prayer, saying to the Lord: "Help me to understand your Word, what it is that you want to tell me in this passage."

— *Meeting with the Youth of Rome*
(April 6, 2006)

THINK ABOUT IT

- How do I read Scripture, and how often? Can I improve?
- Scripture is God's Word: Do I ponder the uniqueness and enormity of this gift?
- I should "knock at the door" of Scripture when I have questions about life.

And beginning with Moses and all the prophets, he interpreted to them in all the Scriptures the things concerning himself.... They said to each other, "Did not our hearts burn within us while he talked to us on the road, while he opened to us the Scriptures?"

LUKE 24:27, 32

REMEMBER

I must read Sacred Scripture as the Word of God, entering into a conversation with God.

36. We Cannot Love If We Do Not Know

How can one love, how can one enter into friendship with someone unknown? Knowledge is an incentive to love, and love stimulates knowledge. This is how it is with Christ too. To find love with Christ, to truly find him as the companion of our lives, we must first of all be acquainted with him.

Like the two disciples who followed him after hearing the words of John the Baptist and asked him timidly, "Rabbi, where are you staying?" they wanted to know him better. It was Jesus himself, talking to his disciples, who made the distinction: "Who do people say that I am," referring to those who knew him from afar, so to speak, by hearsay, and "Who do you say that I am?" referring to those who knew him personally, having lived with him and having truly penetrated his private life, to the point of witnessing his prayer, his dialogue with the Father. Thus, it is also important for us not to reduce ourselves merely to the superficiality of the many who have heard something about him — that he was an important figure, etc. — but to enter into a personal relationship to know him truly. And this demands knowledge of Scripture, especially of the Gospels where the Lord speaks to us. These words are not always easy, but in entering into them, entering into dialogue, knocking at the door of words, saying to the Lord, "Let me in," we truly find words of eternal life, living words for today, as timely as they were then and as they will be in the future. This conversation with the Lord in Scripture must always be a conversation that is not only individual but communal, in the great communion of the Church where Christ is ever present, in the communion of the liturgy, of the very personal encounter with the Holy Eucharist and of the Sacrament of Reconciliation, where the Lord says to me, "I forgive you." And another very important step to take is to help the poor in need, to make time for others. There are many dimensions for entering into knowledge of Jesus.

— *Address to Young People,*
Genoa, Italy (May 18, 2008)

THINK ABOUT IT

- Do I place myself at the core or at the edges of Jesus' life in the world?
- Do I make time for conversation with Jesus?
- Am I growing in my friendship with Jesus?

JUST IMAGINE

Jesus withdrew with his disciples to the sea.

MARK 3:7

To find love with Christ, to truly find him as the companion of my life, I must first of all be acquainted with him.

It is time to reaffirm the importance of prayer in the face of the activism and the growing secularism of many Christians engaged in charitable work. Clearly, the Christian who prays does not claim to be able to change God's plans or correct what he has foreseen. Rather, he seeks an encounter with the Father of Jesus Christ, asking God to be present with the consolation of the Spirit to him and his work. A personal relationship with God and abandonment to his will can prevent man from being demeaned and save him from falling prey to the teaching of fanaticism and terrorism. An authentically religious attitude prevents man from presuming to judge God, accusing him of allowing poverty and failing to have compassion for his creatures. When people claim to build a case against God in defense of man, on whom can they depend when human activity proves powerless?

— *Deus Caritas Est*, n. 37
(encyclical, December 25, 2005)

THINK ABOUT IT

- Do I allow my good deeds and charity to serve as a poor substitute for prayer?
- I need to schedule regular times each day for quiet prayer and spiritual reflection.

- Serving others does not replace the need to give God his due.

In these days he went out to the hills to pray; and all night he continued in prayer to God.

LUKE 6:12

St. Francis de Sales said, "Every one of us needs at least half an hour of prayer each day; except when we're busy, then we need an hour!"

Life is truly always a choice: between honesty and dishonesty, between fidelity and infidelity, between selfishness and altruism, between good and evil. The conclusion of this Gospel passage is incisive and peremptory: "No servant can serve two masters; for either he will hate the one and love the other, or he will be devoted to the one and despise the other." Ultimately, Jesus says, "You cannot serve God and mammon" (Lk 16:13). *Mammon* is a term of Phoenician origin that calls to mind economic security and success in business; we might say that riches are shown as the idol to which everything is sacrificed in order to attain one's own material success; hence, this economic success becomes a person's true god. As a result, it is necessary to make a fundamental decision between God and mammon; it is necessary to choose between the logic of profit as the ultimate criterion for our action, and the logic of sharing and solidarity. If the logic of profit prevails, it widens the gap between the poor and the rich, as well as increasing the ruinous exploitation of the planet. On the other hand, when the logic of sharing and solidarity prevails, it is possible to correct the course and direct it to a fair development for the common good of all. Basically, it is a matter of choosing between selfishness and love, between justice and dishonesty, and ultimately, between God and Satan. If loving Christ and one's brethren is not to be considered as something incidental and superficial but, rather, the true and ultimate purpose of our whole existence, it will be necessary to know how to make basic choices, to be prepared to make radical renouncements, if necessary even to the point of martyrdom. Today, as yesterday, Christian life demands the courage to go against the tide, to love like Jesus, who even went so far as to sacrifice himself on the Cross.

— Homily During Visit to Diocese of
Velletri-Segni, Italy (September 23, 2007)

THINK ABOUT IT

- How, in my work, do I exercise my stewardship over the planet and its resources?
- Do I waste paper or other supplies? Do I waste people's time?
- Am I prepared to renounce profits rather than impoverish people in any way?

JUST IMAGINE

"For what does it profit a man if he gains the whole world and loses or forfeits himself?"

LUKE 9:25

REMEMBER

Christian life demands the courage to go against the tide, to love like Jesus, who even went so far as to sacrifice himself on the Cross.

Do not follow the way of pride but rather that of humility. Go against the tide: do not listen to the interested and persuasive voices that today are peddling on many sides models of life marked by arrogance and violence, by oppression and success at any cost, by appearances, and by *having* at the expense of *being*. How many messages, which reach you especially through the mass media, are targeting you! Be alert! Be critical! Do not follow the wave produced by this powerful, persuasive action. Do not be afraid, dear friends, to prefer the "alternative" routes pointed out by true love: a modest and sound lifestyle; sincere and pure emotional relationships; honest commitment in studies and work; deep concern for the common good. Do not be afraid of seeming different and being criticized for what might seem to be losing or out of fashion; your peers..., especially those who seem more distant from the mindset and values of the Gospel, are crying out to see someone who dares to live according to the fullness of humanity revealed by Jesus Christ.

— *Homily on the Plain of Montorso, Italy*
(September 2, 2007; emphasis added)

- Do I allow myself to be unduly swayed by the desire for human respect?
- Am I a follower or a leader? If a follower, then whom am I following?
- Am I a critical and moderate consumer of the mass media?

JUST IMAGINE

Do not be conformed to this world but be transformed by the renewal of your mind, that you may prove what is the will of God, what is good and acceptable and perfect.

ROMANS 12:2

REMEMBER

Do not be afraid of seeming different and being criticized.

40. How to Take a Sick Day

Suffering is of course repugnant to the human spirit; yet, it is true that when it is accepted with love and compassion and illumined by faith, it becomes a precious opportunity that mysteriously unites one to Christ the Redeemer, the Man of sorrows who on the Cross took upon himself human suffering and death.

With the sacrifice of his life, he redeemed human suffering and made it the fundamental means of salvation.

Dear sick people, entrust to the Lord the hardships and sorrows that you have to face and in his plan they will become a means of purification and redemption for the whole world.

— *Visit to San Matteo Polyclinic,*
Pavia, Italy (April 22, 2007)

THINK ABOUT IT

- Do I offer up my discomforts, or do I waste them by complaining?
- Do I smile for others and try to think of them rather than myself, even when I am suffering?
- Do I view suffering as a means to purification, for myself and for the world?

For as we share abundantly in Christ's sufferings, so through Christ we share abundantly in comfort too. If we are afflicted, it is for your comfort and salvation; and if we are comforted, it is for your comfort, which you experience when you patiently endure the same sufferings that we suffer. Our hope for you is unshaken; for we know that as you share in our sufferings, you will also share in our comfort.

2 CORINTHIANS 1:5-7

REMEMBER

Entrust to the Lord the hardships that have to be faced and they will become a means of purification and redemption for the whole world.

41. Personal Relationship With Christ

Turning now to ourselves, let us ask what this means for us. It means that for us too Christianity is not a new philosophy or a new morality. We are only Christians if we encounter Christ. Of course, he does not show himself to us in this overwhelming, luminous way, as he did to Paul to make him the Apostle to all peoples. But we too can encounter Christ in reading Sacred Scripture, in prayer, in the liturgical life of the Church. We can touch Christ's Heart and feel him touching ours. Only in this personal relationship with Christ, only in this encounter with the Risen One do we truly become Christians. And in this way our reason opens, all Christ's wisdom opens as do all the riches of truth.

Therefore let us pray the Lord to illumine us, to grant us an encounter with his presence in our world, and thus to grant us a lively faith, an open heart and great love for all, which is capable of renewing the world.

— *General Audience* (September 3, 2008)

THINK ABOUT IT

- Does my prayer lead me to a personal encounter with the living Christ?
- Do I listen to the Scriptures and become attentive to God's voice in my life?

■ Being a follower of Christ means that I will grow ever more in my likeness to him.

"You are the salt of the earth; but if salt has lost its taste, how shall its saltiness be restored? It is no longer good for anything except to be thrown out and trodden under foot by men.

"You are the light of the world. A city set on a hill cannot be hid. Nor do men light a lamp and put it under a bushel, but on a stand, and it gives light to all in the house. Let your light so shine before men, that they may see your good works and give glory to your Father who is in heaven."

MATTHEW 5:13-16

Faith draws me into a close personal relationship with Jesus Christ, who became like me so that I might become more and more like him.

Faith in Christ brought all Augustine's seeking to fulfillment, but fulfillment in the sense that he always remained on the way. Indeed, he tells us: even in eternity our seeking will not be completed, it will be an eternal adventure, the discovery of new greatness, new beauty.

He interpreted the words of the Psalm, "Seek his face continually," and said: this is true for eternity; and the beauty of eternity is that it is not a static reality but immense progress in the immense beauty of God.

— *Address to Representatives of the World of Culture, Pavia, Italy* (April 22, 2007)

THINK ABOUT IT

- Do I see my professional and natural curiosity as a drive toward God?
- Are my beliefs about heaven true motivations for living well on earth? Do I see heaven as "an eternal adventure"?
- Do I seek God continually, realizing that I can never know enough of him?

For every one who asks receives, and he who seeks
finds, and to him who knocks it will be opened.

MATTHEW 7:8

Even in eternity, my seeking will not be completed;
it will be an eternal adventure.

So it is that day after day the Church offers us the possibility of walking in the company of saints. Hans Urs von Balthasar wrote that the saints constitute the most important message of the Gospel, its actualization in daily life, and therefore represent for us a real means of access to Jesus....

Every day of the year affords us an opportunity to familiarize ourselves with our heavenly patrons. Their human and spiritual experience shows that holiness is not a luxury, it is not a privilege for the few, an impossible goal for an ordinary person; it is actually the common destiny of all men called to be children of God, the universal vocation of all the baptized. Holiness is offered to all.

— *General Audience*
(August 20, 2008)

THINK ABOUT IT

- Do I study the lives of the saints and see them as models of holiness for my life?
- Am I attracted to particular saints who can inspire me to seek perfection?
- Do I rely on the intercession of the saints in times of need?

To the Church of God which is at Corinth, to those sanctified in Christ Jesus, called to be saints together with all those who in every place call on the name of our Lord Jesus Christ, both their Lord and ours:

Grace to you and peace from God our Father and the Lord Jesus Christ.

1 CORINTHIANS 1:2-3

All Christians in any state or walk of life are called to the fullness of Christian life; all are called to holiness (see CCC 2013).

44. Ready With a Reason

We know well that this choice of faith and of following Christ is never easy. Instead, it is always opposed and controversial. The Church remains, therefore, a "sign of contradiction" in the footsteps of her Master (cf. Lk 2:34), even in our time.

But we do not lose heart because of this. On the contrary, we must always be ready to give a response (*apo-logia*) to whoever asks us the reason (*logos*) for our hope, as the First Letter of St. Peter (3:15) invites us.... We must answer "with gentleness and reverence," with a "clear conscience" (3:15-16), with that gentle power that comes from union with Christ.

We must do it full-time, on the level of thought and action, of personal behavior and public witness.

— *Address to National Ecclesial Convention,*
Verona, Italy (October 19, 2006)

THINK ABOUT IT

- I must avoid sin so that my witness will be credible.
- I should never expect people to be impressed by my witness. In fact, I should expect opposition.
- Still, I should strive to speak persuasively, reasonably, and gently.

"Remember the word that I said to you, 'A servant is not greater than his master.' If they persecuted me, they will persecute you; if they kept my word, they will keep yours also."

JOHN 15:20

REMEMBER

Following Christ is never easy. It is always opposed and controversial.

Practical activity will always be insufficient, unless it visibly expresses a love for man, a love nourished by an encounter with Christ. My deep personal sharing in the needs and sufferings of others becomes a sharing of my very self with them: if my gift is not to prove a source of humiliation, I must give to others not only something that is my own, but my very self; I must be personally present in my gift.

— *Deus Caritas Est*, n. 34
(encyclical, December 25, 2005)

THINK ABOUT IT

■ Do I act kindly in order to be recognized by others? Or do I act for love's sake?

■ Am I upset with others when they fail to thank me?

■ Am I willing to share my time and become personally involved in the lives of those who need help?

JUST IMAGINE

"Beware of practicing your piety before men in order to be seen by them; for then you will have no reward from your Father who is in heaven.

"Thus, when you give alms, sound no trumpet before you, as the hypocrites do in the synagogues and in the streets, that they may be praised by men. Truly, I say to you, they have their reward. But when you give alms, do not let your left hand know what your right hand is doing, so that your alms may be in secret; and your Father who sees in secret will reward you."

MATTHEW 6:1-4

REMEMBER

God knows the motivations of my heart and rejoices in the selfless servant.

Dear friends..., we must rediscover the joy of Christian Sundays. We must proudly rediscover the privilege of sharing in the Eucharist, which is the sacrament of the renewed world.

Christ's Resurrection happened on the first day of the week, which in the Scriptures is the day of the world's creation. For this very reason Sunday was considered by the early Christian community as the day on which the new world began, the one on which, with Christ's victory over death, the new creation began.

As they gathered round the Eucharistic table, the community was taking shape as a new people of God. St. Ignatius of Antioch described Christians as "having attained new hope" and presented them as people "who lived in accordance with Sunday."

... It is this that gives rise to our prayer: that we too, Christians of today, will rediscover an awareness of the crucial importance of the Sunday Celebration and will know how to draw from participation in the Eucharist the necessary dynamism for a new commitment to proclaiming to the world Christ *"our peace"* (Eph 2:14). Amen!

— *Homily, National Eucharistic Congress, Bari, Italy* (May 29, 2005; emphasis in original)

- Do I use Sundays as a time for renewal and prayer?
- Is my workweek ordered toward the Lord's Day, and does Sunday provide direction for the following week?
- How important is Sunday to me? Would anyone say that I "live in accordance" with it?

JUST IMAGINE

And after six days Jesus took with him Peter and James and John his brother, and led them up a high mountain apart.

MATTHEW 17:1

REMEMBER

I must rediscover the joy of Christian Sundays.

47. The Happiness You Desire

The happiness you have a right to enjoy has a name and a face: it is Jesus of Nazareth, hidden in the Eucharist. Only he gives the fullness of life to humanity! With Mary, say your own "yes" to God, for he wishes to give himself to you.

I repeat today what I said at the beginning of my Pontificate: "If we let Christ into our lives, we lose nothing, nothing, absolutely nothing of what makes life free, beautiful, and great. No! Only in this friendship are the doors of life opened wide. Only in this friendship is the great potential of human existence truly revealed. Only in this friendship do we experience beauty and liberation."

Be completely convinced of this: Christ takes from you nothing that is beautiful and great, but brings everything to perfection for the glory of God, the happiness of men and women, and the salvation of the world.

— *Address, World Youth Day,*
Cologne, Germany (August 18, 2005)

THINK ABOUT IT

- The Eucharist contains all the happiness I could wish for myself.
- I must cultivate a friendship with Jesus, speaking with him more often.

- By choosing Christ, I lose nothing and I gain everything.

"You are my friends if you do what I command you. No longer do I call you servants, for the servant does not know what his master is doing; but I have called you friends, for all that I have heard from my Father I have made known to you."

JOHN 15:14-15

If I let Christ into my life, I lose absolutely nothing of what makes life free, beautiful, and great.

In vast areas of the world today there is a strange forgetfulness of God. It seems as if everything would be just the same even without him.

But at the same time there is a feeling of frustration, a sense of dissatisfaction with everyone and everything.

People tend to exclaim: "This cannot be what life is about!" Indeed not. And so, together with forgetfulness of God there is a kind of new explosion of religion. I have no wish to discredit all the manifestations of this phenomenon. There may be sincere joy in the discovery. But to tell the truth, religion often becomes almost a consumer product. People choose what they like, and some are even able to make a profit from it.

But religion sought on a "do-it-yourself" basis cannot ultimately help us. It may be comfortable, but at times of crisis we are left to ourselves.

Help people to discover the true star which points out the way to us: Jesus Christ! Let us seek to know him better and better, so as to be able to guide others to him with conviction.

— *Homily, World Youth Day,*
Cologne, Germany (August 21, 2005)

- Which friends and co-workers have forgotten God? How can I help them "remember"?
- Is there any do-it-yourself element in my faith? How can I root it out?
- I will seek to know Jesus better and better, and lead others to him.

Abide in me, and I in you ... I am the vine, you are the branches. He who abides in me, and I in him, he it is that bears much fruit, for apart from me you can do nothing.

JOHN 15:4, 5

Religion sought on a "do-it-yourself" basis cannot ultimately help me.

49. False Gods I: Things

Material possessions, in themselves, are good. We would not survive for long without money, clothing, and shelter. We must eat in order to stay alive. Yet if we are greedy, if we refuse to share what we have with the hungry and the poor, then we make our possessions into a false god. How many voices in our materialist society tell us that happiness is to be found by acquiring as many possessions and luxuries as we can! But this is to make possessions into a false god. Instead of bringing life, they bring death.

— *Address to Disadvantaged Youth, Sydney, Australia* (July 18, 2008)

THINK ABOUT IT

- Do I thank God — every day — for the good things I have?
- Do I buy things I don't need with money that's best spent elsewhere?
- Is giving to charity among the top priorities of my budget?

JUST IMAGINE

"The land of a rich man brought forth plentifully; and he thought to himself, 'What shall I do, for I have nowhere to store my crops?' And he said, 'I will do this: I will pull down my barns, and build larger ones; and there I will store all my grain and my goods. And I will say to my soul, Soul, you have ample goods laid up for many years; take your ease, eat, drink, be merry.' "But God said to him, 'Fool! This night your soul is required of you; and the things you have prepared, whose will they be?'"

LUKE 12:16-20

REMEMBER

If I am greedy, if I refuse to share what I have with the hungry and the poor, then I make my possessions into a false god.

50. False Gods II: "Love"

Authentic love is obviously something good. Without it, life would hardly be worth living. It fulfills our deepest need, and when we love, we become most fully ourselves, most fully human. But how easily it can be made into a false god! People often think they are being loving when actually they are being possessive or manipulative. People sometimes treat others as objects to satisfy their own needs rather than as persons to be loved and cherished. How easy it is to be deceived by the many voices in our society that advocate a permissive approach to sexuality, without regard for modesty, self-respect, or the moral values that bring quality to human relationships! This is worship of a false god. Instead of bringing life, it brings death.

— Address to Disadvantaged Youth,
Sydney, Australia (July 18, 2008)

THINK ABOUT IT

- I must never treat another person as an object.
- Even the greatest of earthly goods — even human love — must be subordinated to God.
- Is my approach to sexuality marked by modesty, self-respect, and moral values?

"This is my commandment, that you love one another as I have loved you."

JOHN 15:12

REMEMBER

People often think they are being loving when actually they are being possessive or manipulative.

51. False Gods III: Power

The power God has given us to shape the world around us is obviously something good. Used properly and responsibly, it enables us to transform people's lives. Yet how tempting it can be to grasp at power for its own sake, to seek to dominate others or to exploit the natural environment for selfish purposes! This is to make power into a false god. Instead of bringing life, it brings death.

The cult of material possessions, the cult of possessive love, and the cult of power often lead people to attempt to play God; to try and seize total control, with no regard for the wisdom or the commandments that God has made known to us. This is the path that leads towards death. By contrast, worship of the one true God means recognizing in him the source of all goodness, entrusting ourselves to him, opening ourselves to the healing power of his grace and obeying his commandments; that is the way to choose life.

— *Address to Disadvantaged Youth, Sydney, Australia* (July 18, 2008)

THINK ABOUT IT

■ Do I seek to manipulate others for my own personal gain or benefit?

- Does the desire for success, prestige, or wealth lead me to engage in practices or behaviors that diminish or take advantage of others?
- Do I cherish and protect the goods of the earth by being responsible and ethical in their use?

JUST IMAGINE

See, I have set before you this day life and good, death and evil. If you obey the commandments of the LORD your God which I command you this day, by loving the LORD your God, by walking in his ways, and by keeping his commandments and his statutes and his ordinances, then you shall live and multiply, and the LORD your God will bless you in the land which you are entering to take possession of it. But if your heart turns away, and you will not hear, but are drawn away to worship other gods and serve them, I declare to you this day that you shall perish.

DEUTERONOMY 30:15-18

REMEMBER

I ought to use the things of this world as though I used them not, and own them as though I owned them not.

52. God's Encouragement

I need you" — "You can do it!" How good it feels to hear words like these! In their human simplicity, they unwittingly point us to the God who has called each of us into being and given us a personal task, the God who needs each of us and awaits our response. Jesus called men and women, and gave them the courage needed to embark on a great undertaking, one to which, by themselves, they would never have dared to aspire. To allow oneself to be called, to make a decision and then to set out on a path — without the usual questions about whether it is useful or profitable — this attitude will naturally bring healing in its wake.

— *Meeting with Voluntary Associations, Vienna, Austria* (September 9, 2007)

THINK ABOUT IT

- Every individual shares in the call to holiness and the mission to evangelize the world.
- Do I discern God's call and strive for perfection in my particular state of life?
- Only life in the Holy Spirit and the Church fulfills the human vocation and leads to complete happiness.

"You, therefore, must be perfect, as your heavenly Father is perfect."

MATTHEW 5:48

St. Paul reminded me to desire the higher gifts, to pursue the more excellent way, the way of love, which surpasses everything.

53. The Ministry of Angels

I entrust you in a special way to the loving protection of these heavenly spirits that the Lord has set beside us. May it be they who guide and accompany you on the path of the good.

— *Address to Personnel of the Pontifical Villas, Castel Gandolfo* (October 1, 2007)

THINK ABOUT IT

- Angels are special servants and messengers of God.
- Do I believe in the presence of angels as special protectors from God?
- Do I invoke the blessing of my guardian angel each day?

JUST IMAGINE

"See that you do not despise one of these little ones; for I tell you that in heaven their angels always behold the face of my Father."

MATTHEW 18:10

REMEMBER

From its beginning until death, human life is surrounded by the angels' watchful care and intercession (see CCC 336).

But then the question arises: do we really want this — to live eternally? Perhaps many people reject the faith today simply because they do not find the prospect of eternal life attractive. What they desire is not eternal life at all, but this present life, for which faith in eternal life seems something of an impediment. To continue living forever — endlessly — appears more like a curse than a gift. Death, admittedly, one would wish to postpone for as long as possible. But to live always, without end — this, all things considered, can only be monotonous and ultimately unbearable. This is precisely the point made, for example, by St. Ambrose, one of the Church Fathers...: "Death was not part of nature; it became part of nature. God did not decree death from the beginning; he prescribed it as a remedy. Human life, because of sin... began to experience the burden of wretchedness in unremitting labor and unbearable sorrow. There had to be a limit to its evils; death had to restore what life had forfeited. Without the assistance of grace, immortality is more of a burden than a blessing." A little earlier, Ambrose had said: "Death is, then, no cause for mourning, for it is the cause of mankind's salvation."

— *Spe Salvi*, n. 10
(encyclical, November 30, 2007)

- Death does not end life, but changes it. When the body of our earthly dwelling lies in death, we gain an everlasting dwelling place in heaven.
- When I grieve the loss of loved ones, am I able to rejoice in their gain of eternal life?
- Do I pray for the grace to accept my own death with trust in God?

JUST IMAGINE

Who shall separate us from the love of Christ? Shall tribulation, or distress, or persecution, or famine, or nakedness, or peril, or sword? As it is written,

> "For your sake we are being killed all the day long;
> we are regarded as sheep to be slaughtered."

No, in all these things we are more than conquerors through him who loved us. For I am sure that neither death, nor life, nor angels, nor principalities, nor things present, nor things to come, nor powers, nor height, nor depth, nor anything else in all creation, will be able to separate us from the love of God in Christ Jesus our Lord.

ROMANS 8:35-39

REMEMBER

How great will my happiness be when I see God face-to-face!

55. Praying for the Dead

The souls of the departed can, however, receive "solace and refreshment" through the Eucharist, prayer, and almsgiving. The belief that love can reach into the afterlife, that reciprocal giving and receiving is possible, in which our affection for one another continues beyond the limits of death — this has been a fundamental conviction of Christianity throughout the ages and it remains a source of comfort today. Who would not feel the need to convey to their departed loved ones a sign of kindness, a gesture of gratitude, or even a request for pardon?

— *Spe Salvi*, n. 48
(encyclical, November 30, 2007)

THINK ABOUT IT

- Do I remember to pray for the souls of the faithful departed and offer Masses for them?
- Do I offer acts of penance for the remission of the sins of my loved ones who have died?
- We are joined to the communion of saints in spiritual bonds that remain unbroken across space and time.

JUST IMAGINE

Blessed be the God and Father of our Lord Jesus Christ! By his great mercy we have been born anew to a living hope through the resurrection of Jesus Christ from the dead, and to an inheritance which is imperishable, undefiled, and unfading, kept in heaven for you, who by God's power are guarded through faith for a salvation ready to be revealed in the last time. In this you rejoice, though now for a little while you may have to suffer various trials, so that the genuineness of your faith, more precious than gold which though perishable is tested by fire, may redound to praise and glory and honor at the revelation of Jesus Christ. Without having seen him you love him; though you do not now see him you believe in him and rejoice with unutterable and exalted joy. As the outcome of your faith you obtain the salvation of your souls.

1 PETER 1:3-9

REMEMBER

From the beginning, the Church has honored the blessed memory of the dead and offered prayers for their purification so that they might attain the fullness of eternal life.

56. Working for Unity

Even in the face of difficulties and divisions, Christians cannot be resigned nor yield to discouragement. The Lord asks this of us: to persevere in prayer in order to keep alive the flame of faith, love, and hope which nourishes the desire for full unity. "*Ut unum sint*!" ["that they may be one"] says the Lord. May Christ's invitation always resound in our hearts, an invitation I was able to relaunch on my recent Apostolic Journey in the United States of America, when I referred to the centrality of prayer in the ecumenical movement. In this epoch of globalization and at the same time of fragmentation, "without [prayer], ecumenical structures, institutions, and programs would be deprived of their heart and soul." Let us give thanks to the Lord for the goals reached in ecumenical dialogue thanks to the Holy Spirit's action; let us be docile, listening to his voice so that our hearts, filled with hope, may continuously seek the path that leads to the full communion of all Christ's disciples.

— *General Audience*
(May 7, 2008)

THINK ABOUT IT

■ Do I participate in prayer and conversation that build up the unity of all Christians?

- Do I fall prey to gossip, slander, and bias that can cause division and hatred?
- Am I able to say I am sorry when I hurt someone? Do I immediately accept the apologies of others?

JUST IMAGINE

"I do not pray for these only, but also for those who believe in me through their word, that they may all be one; even as you, Father, are in me, and I in you, that they also may be in us, so that the world may believe that you have sent me. The glory which you have given me I have given to them, that they may be one even as we are one, I in them and you in me, that they may become perfectly one, so that the world may know that you have sent me and have loved them even as you have loved me."

JOHN 17:20-23

REMEMBER

Even in the face of difficulties and divisions, Christians cannot be resigned nor yield to discouragement.

Christianity's new worship includes and transfigures every aspect of life: "Whether you eat or drink, or whatever you do, do all to the glory of God" (1 Cor 10:31). Christians, in all their actions, are called to offer true worship to God. Here the intrinsically Eucharistic nature of Christian life begins to take shape. The Eucharist, since it embraces the concrete, everyday existence of the believer, makes possible, day by day, the progressive transfiguration of all those called by grace to reflect the image of the Son of God (cf. Rom 8:29ff). There is nothing authentically human — our thoughts and affections, our words and deeds — that does not find in the Sacrament of the Eucharist the form it needs to be lived to the full.

— *Sacramentum Caritatis*, n. 71
(apostolic exhortation, February 22, 2007)

THINK ABOUT IT

- The Eucharist is the most powerful prayer of thanksgiving to God.
- Do we offer every thought and action to the greater glory of God, who made us and gave us salvation through Christ?
- The grace of the Eucharist works inside our hearts to change us into the person God wants us to be.

And let the peace of Christ rule in your hearts, to which indeed you were called in the one body. And be thankful. Let the word of Christ dwell in you richly, as you teach and admonish one another in all wisdom, and as you sing psalms and hymns and spiritual songs with thankfulness in your hearts to God. And whatever you do, in word or deed, do everything in the name of the Lord Jesus, giving thanks to God the Father through him.

COLOSSIANS 3:15-17

REMEMBER

The Eucharist is the source and summit of the whole of Christian life, the goal toward which I strive and the inspiration that enables me to get there.

58. Adoration of the Blessed Sacrament

Go to ... encounter [Jesus] in the Blessed Eucharist, go to adore him in the churches, kneeling before the tabernacle: Jesus will fill you with his love and will reveal to you the thoughts of his heart. If you listen to him, you will feel ever more deeply the joy of belonging to his Mystical Body, the Church, which is the family of his disciples held close by the bond of unity and love.

— *Message to Young Catholics of The Netherlands*
(November 21, 2005)

THINK ABOUT IT

- Do I show reverence for the Blessed Sacrament when I enter and leave the church? Do I genuflect?
- Might I make a visit to the tabernacle on my way to or from work, or during a break?
- Do I cultivate a strong belief in Jesus' real presence in the Sacrament?

JUST IMAGINE

For I received from the Lord what I also delivered to you, that the Lord Jesus on the night when he was betrayed took bread, and when he had given thanks, he broke it, and said, "This is my body which is for you. Do this in remembrance of me." In the same way also the chalice, after supper, saying, "This chalice is the new covenant in my blood. Do this, as often as you drink it, in remembrance of me." For as often as you eat this bread and drink the chalice, you proclaim the Lord's death until he comes.

1 CORINTHIANS 11:23-26

REMEMBER

The *Catechism* tells me that the Church and the world have a great need for Eucharistic worship: "Jesus awaits us in this sacrament of love.... Let our adoration never cease" (CCC 1380; Pope John Paul II, *Dominicae Cenae*, n. 3).

59. Building Up a Spiritual Reserve

There is always a certain tension between what I absolutely have to do and what spiritual reserves I must have. I always see it in St. Augustine, who complains about this in his preaching ...: "I long to live with the Word of God from morning to night but I have to be with you." Augustine nonetheless finds this balance by being always available but also by keeping for himself moments of prayer and meditation on the Sacred Word, because otherwise he would no longer be able to say anything.

— Meeting with the Clergy of Rome
(February 22, 2007)

THINK ABOUT IT

- Do I make time to build up my spiritual reserves through prayer?
- Do I engage in spiritual works of mercy that increase God's life in me?
- Do I deepen my understanding of God's Word through study and meditation?

JUST IMAGINE

"But when you pray, go into your room and shut the door and pray to your Father who is in secret; and your Father who sees in secret will reward you."

MATTHEW 6:6

I cannot give to someone else what I do not first possess.

60. Concern for Others

We should recall that no man is an island, entire of itself. Our lives are involved with one another, through innumerable interactions they are linked together. No one lives alone. No one sins alone. No one is saved alone. The lives of others continually spill over into mine: in what I think, say, do, and achieve. And conversely, my life spills over into that of others: for better and for worse. So my prayer for another is not something extraneous to that person, something external, not even after death.... As Christians we should never limit ourselves to asking: how can I save myself? We should also ask: what can I do in order that others may be saved and that for them too the star of hope may rise? Then I will have done my utmost for my own personal salvation as well.

— *Spe Salvi*, n. 48
(encyclical, November 30, 2007)

THINK ABOUT IT

- I will share my influence and my worldly goods, especially with those who are most in need.
- I am able to see in others the face of Christ and help them to experience the tenderness of Christ through me.

- Am I aware that the people I meet are heaven-sent for the sake of my salvation?

"Then the righteous will answer him, 'Lord, when did we see you hungry and feed you, or thirsty and give you drink? And when did we see you a stranger and welcome you, or naked and clothe you? And when did we see you sick or in prison and visit you?' And the King will answer them, 'Truly, I say to you, as you did it to one of the least of these my brethren, you did it to me.'"

MATTHEW 25:37-40

No one can outdo the generosity of God. Those who give for the good of others will receive far more in return.

61. Friendship in Christ

Love of neighbor is thus shown to be possible in the way proclaimed by the Bible, by Jesus. It consists in the very fact that, in God and with God, I love even the person whom I do not like or even know. This can only take place on the basis of an intimate encounter with God, an encounter which has become a communion of will, even affecting my feelings. Then I learn to look on this other person not simply with my eyes and my feelings, but from the perspective of Jesus Christ. His friend is my friend.

— *Deus Caritas Est*, n. 18
(encyclical, December 25, 2005)

THINK ABOUT IT

■ Faith binds us to one another in ties that are deeper than blood; we are brothers and sisters in Christ.

■ Do I work to overcome the prejudices that so often lead to hatred, discrimination, and division?

■ Am I able to set aside grievances and hurts, and pray and work for the ultimate good of those I don't like?

"But I say to you, Love your enemies and pray for those who persecute you, so that you may be sons of your Father who is in heaven; for he makes his sun rise on the evil and on the good, and sends rain on the just and on the unjust. For if you love those who love you, what reward have you? Do not even the tax collectors do the same? And if you salute only your brethren, what more are you doing than others? Do not even the Gentiles do the same? You, therefore, must be perfect, as your heavenly Father is perfect."

MATTHEW 5:44-48

REMEMBER

In God and with God, I love even the person I do not like. I look on this other person from the perspective of Jesus. His friend is my friend.

Conscious of this new vital principle which the Eucharist imparts to the Christian, the Synod Fathers reaffirmed the importance of the Sunday obligation for all the faithful, viewing it as a wellspring of authentic freedom enabling them to live each day in accordance with what they celebrated on "the Lord's Day." The life of faith is endangered when we lose the desire to share in the celebration of the Eucharist and its commemoration of the paschal victory. Participating in the Sunday liturgical assembly with all our brothers and sisters, with whom we form one body in Jesus Christ, is demanded by our Christian conscience and at the same time it forms that conscience. To lose a sense of Sunday as the Lord's Day, a day to be sanctified, is symptomatic of the loss of an authentic sense of Christian freedom, the freedom of the children of God....

On the Lord's Day, then, it is fitting that Church groups should organize, around Sunday Mass, the activities of the Christian community: social gatherings, programs for the faith formation of children, young people and adults, pilgrimages, charitable works, and different moments of prayer.... We need to remember that it is Sunday itself that is meant to be kept holy, lest it end up as a day "empty of God."

— *Sacramentum Caritatis*, n. 73 (apostolic exhortation, February 22, 2007)

- The Third Commandment obliges us to keep holy the Lord's Day.
- What can I do to enrich my Sunday so that it can become a balance of worship, restful reflection, and personal spiritual renewal?
- How do I help to make Sunday different from the rest of the week and provide my family an opportunity to grow in an appreciation of God?

JUST IMAGINE

And on the seventh day God finished his work which he had done, and he rested on the seventh day from all his work which he had done. So God blessed the seventh day and hallowed it, because on it God rested from all his work which he had done in creation.

GENESIS 2:2-3

REMEMBER

Sunday brings everyday work to a halt, brings a respite from the busyness of daily life, and lifts my mind and heart to God.

63. Confirmed in the Spirit

Meditate on the importance of the Sacrament of Confirmation, which you have received and which leads you into a mature faith life. It is vital for you to understand this sacrament more and more in order to evaluate the quality and depth of your faith and to reinforce it. The Holy Spirit enables you to approach the Mystery of God; he makes you understand who God is. He invites you to see in your neighbors the brothers and sisters whom God has given you, in order to live with them in human and spiritual fellowship — in other words, to live within the Church. By revealing who the crucified and risen Lord is for us, he impels you to bear witness to Christ.

— *Address to Young People,*
Paris (September 12, 2008)

THINK ABOUT IT

- Confirmation seals me with the gift of the Spirit and strengthens me for service to the Body of Christ.
- Do I pray for the gifts of the Spirit to enrich my life — wisdom, understanding, knowledge, fortitude, counsel, piety, and fear of the Lord?
- Is my life a true and powerful witness to my commitment to Jesus Christ and his Gospel?

And when they had prayed, the place in which they were gathered together was shaken; and they were all filled with the Holy Spirit and spoke the word of God with boldness.

Now the company of those who believed was of one heart and soul, and no one said that any of the things which he possessed was his own, but they had everything in common. And with great power the apostles gave their testimony to the resurrection of the Lord Jesus, and great grace was upon them all.

ACTS 4:31-33

REMEMBER

Confirmation gives me the Spirit's power to spread and defend the faith by word and deed, to profess Christ boldly and never be ashamed of the Cross.

Indeed, it is to him and his grace alone that we owe what we are as Christians. Since nothing and no one can replace him, it is necessary that we pay homage to nothing and no one else but him. No idol should pollute our spiritual universe or otherwise, instead of enjoying the freedom acquired, we will relapse into a humiliating form of slavery....

Our radical belonging to Christ and the fact that "we are in him" must imbue in us an attitude of total trust and immense joy. In short, we must indeed exclaim with St Paul: "If God is for us, who is against us?" (Rom 8:31). And the reply is that nothing and no one "will be able to separate us from the love of God in Christ Jesus our Lord" (Rom 8:39). Our Christian life, therefore, stands on the soundest and safest rock one can imagine. And from it we draw all our energy, precisely as the Apostle wrote: "I can do all things in him who strengthens me" (Phil 4:13).

— *General Audience* (November 8, 2006)

THINK ABOUT IT

- Grace is our sharing in the life of God; it is the Holy Spirit at work in us.
- Do I work to increase the grace that is in me through prayer and good deeds?

- Do I evidence my life of grace by the fruits of the Spirit — charity, joy, peace, patience, kindness, goodness, generosity, gentleness, faithfulness, modesty, self-control, and chastity?

When you were slaves of sin, you were free in regard to righteousness. But then what return did you get from the things of which you are now ashamed? The end of those things is death. But now that you have been set free from sin and have become slaves of God, the return you get is sanctification and its end, eternal life. For the wages of sin is death, but the free gift of God is eternal life in Christ Jesus our Lord.

ROMANS 6:20-23

Asked if she knew whether she was in God's grace, St. Joan of Arc replied: "If I am not, may it please God to put me in it; if I am, may it please God to keep me there."

For Christians, the Cross signifies God's wisdom and his infinite love revealed in the saving gift of Christ, crucified and risen for the life of the world, and in particular for the life of each and every one of you. May this discovery of a God who became man out of love — this amazing discovery lead you to respect and venerate the Cross! It is not only the symbol of your life in God and your salvation, but also — as you will understand — the silent witness of human suffering and the unique and priceless expression of all our hopes.... I know that venerating the Cross can sometimes bring mockery and even persecution. The Cross in some way seems to threaten our human security, yet above all else, it also proclaims God's grace and confirms our salvation. This evening, I entrust you with the Cross of Christ. The Holy Spirit will enable you to understand its mysteries of love.

— *Address to Young People,*
Paris (September 12, 2008)

THINK ABOUT IT

■ Do I gaze on the Cross as the Tree of Life upon which Jesus saved me from my sins?

- Do I willingly take up my crosses each day and walk in the footsteps of Jesus, with patient endurance?
- Am I willing to lay down my life each day in service to others, in imitation of the Crucified One?

JUST IMAGINE

And he said to all, "If any man would come after me, let him deny himself and take up his cross daily and follow me. For whoever would save his life will lose it; and whoever loses his life for my sake, he will save it. For what does it profit a man if he gains the whole world and loses or forfeits himself? For whoever is ashamed of me and of my words, of him will the Son of man be ashamed when he comes in his glory and the glory of the Father and of the holy angels."

LUKE 9:23-26

REMEMBER

The Sign of the Cross marks me with the imprint of Christ and calls me to the same self-giving for the sake of others.

Conversion thus entails placing oneself humbly at the school of Jesus and walking meekly in his footsteps. In this regard the words with which he himself points out the conditions for being his true disciples are enlightening. After affirming, "Whoever would save his life will lose it; and whoever loses his life for my sake and the Gospel's will save it," he adds: "For what does it profit a man, to gain the whole world and forfeit his life?" (Mk 8:35-36). To what extent does a life that is totally spent in achieving success, longing for prestige and seeking commodities to the point of excluding God from one's horizon, truly lead to happiness? Can true happiness exist when God is left out of consideration? Experience shows that we are not happy because our material expectations and needs are satisfied. In fact, the only joy that fills the human heart is that which comes from God: indeed, we stand in need of infinite joy. Neither daily concerns nor life's difficulties succeed in extinguishing the joy that is born from friendship with God. Jesus' invitation to take up one's cross and follow him may at first sight seem harsh and contrary to what we hope for, mortifying our desire for personal fulfillment.

— *General Audience*
(February 6, 2008)

- Do I seek constant conversion of heart through prayer and acts of penance?
- Am I consumed at times with the things of this world, especially a desire for more things?
- Do I reflect on the longings of my heart and bring that yearning to God where it alone can be satisfied?

JUST IMAGINE

"Do not lay up for yourselves treasures on earth, where moth and rust consume and where thieves break in and steal, but lay up for yourselves treasures in heaven, where neither moth nor rust consumes and where thieves do not break in and steal. For where your treasure is, there will your heart be also."

MATTHEW 6:19-21

REMEMBER

We are a work in progress, and conversion of heart takes time and trust in God's grace.

The Church asks the faithful ... to receive the Sacrament of Penance, which is like a sort of death and resurrection for each one of us ... because it offers us the possibility of giving our life a fresh start and of truly having a new beginning in the joy of the Risen One and in the communion of the forgiveness that he gives us.

Aware that we are sinners but trusting in divine mercy, let us be reconciled by Christ, to enjoy more intensely the joy that he communicates with his Resurrection. The forgiveness which Christ gives to us in the Sacrament of Penance is a source of interior and exterior peace and makes us apostles of peace in a world where divisions, suffering and the tragedies of injustice, hatred and violence and the inability to be reconciled to one another in order to start again with a sincere pardon, unfortunately continue.

— *General Audience* (April 12, 2006)

THINK ABOUT IT

- Do I approach confession with dread and anxiety, or do I experience it as a gift of God's mercy?
- Am I able to make an examination of conscience each day and understand my need for God's forgiveness?

- Do I understand that the Sacrament of Confession heals any separation from God and the Church?

Jesus said to them again, "Peace be with you. As the Father has sent me, even so I send you." And when he had said this, he breathed on them, and said to them, "Receive the Holy Spirit. If you forgive the sins of any, they are forgiven; if you retain the sins of any, they are retained.

JOHN 20:21-23

What joy there is in heaven when even one sinner returns to God.

Voluntary work is not only "doing": it is first and foremost a way of being that stems from the heart, from a grateful approach to life, and impels one to "give back" and to share with one's neighbor the gifts received. In this perspective, I wanted once again to encourage the volunteer culture.

The volunteer's action should not be seen as a "stop-gap" intervention for the state and public institutions, but rather as a complementary, always necessary, presence to keep attention to the lowliest alive and to further a personalized style in interventions.

Therefore, everyone can be a volunteer worker: even the poorest and most underprivileged person has certainly much to share with others by making his own contribution to building the civilization of love.

— *General Audience* (September 12, 2007)

THINK ABOUT IT

- In giving my time, am I giving to Christ?
- Do I strive to see God's human face in those I serve?
- Do I lift up the needs of the poor in prayer?

"Blessed are the poor in spirit, for theirs is the kingdom of heaven.

Blessed are those who mourn, for they shall be comforted.

Blessed are the meek, for they shall inherit the earth.

Blessed are those who hunger and thirst for righteousness, for they shall be satisfied.

Blessed are the merciful, for they shall obtain mercy.

Blessed are the pure in heart, for they shall see God.

Blessed are the peacemakers, for they shall be called sons of God."

MATTHEW 5:3-9

REMEMBER

Jesus has a special love for the poor and the downtrodden of this world — and those who follow Him must as well.

"My help shall come from the Lord, who made heaven and earth" (Ps 121:2).

There are also similar things in our pilgrimage through life. We see the high places that spread out before us as a promise of life: wealth, power, prestige, the easy life. These high places are temptations, for they truly seem like the promise of life. But with our faith we realize that this is not true and that these high places are not life. True life, true help, comes from the Lord. And we turn our gaze, therefore, to the true high places, to the true mountain: Christ.

— *General Audience*
(May 4, 2005)

THINK ABOUT IT

- Do I indulge — even slightly — temptations to greed, power, lust, etc.?
- Do I seek, through prayer, the help of God's grace in my weakness?
- Do I struggle to overcome temptations in a sustained and disciplined way?

JUST IMAGINE

Again, the devil took him to a very high mountain, and showed him all the kingdoms of the world and the glory of them; and he said to him, "All these I will give you, if you will fall down and worship me." Then Jesus said to him, "Begone, Satan! For it is written,

> 'You shall worship the Lord your God
> and him only shall you serve.'"
>
> Matthew 4:8-10

REMEMBER

Fortitude strengthens us to resist temptations and overcome obstacles in the moral life.

Here, the communion of love that binds the Son to the Father and to men and women is at the same time the model and source of the fraternal communion that must unite disciples with one another: "Love one another *as* I have loved you" (Jn 15:12; cf. 13:34); "that they may all be one ... even *as* we are one" (Jn 17:21-22). Hence, it is communion of men and women with the Trinitarian God and communion of men and women with one another.

... Thus, this twofold communion with God and with one another is inseparable. Wherever communion with God, which is communion with the Father, the Son, and the Holy Spirit, is destroyed, the root and source of our communion with one another is destroyed. And wherever we do not live communion among ourselves, communion with the Trinitarian God is not alive and true either, as we have heard.

— *General Audience* (March 29, 2006; emphasis in original)

THINK ABOUT IT

- Do I seek common ground with people I dislike?
- Am I able to set aside anger, hurt, distrust, and envy in working for the good of others?

■ Do I understand that in loving another, I am loving God, and in turning away from another, I am turning away from God?

We love, because he first loved us. If any one says, "I love God," and hates his brother, he is a liar; for he who does not love his brother whom he has seen, cannot love God whom he has not seen. And this commandment we have from him, that he who loves God should love his brother also.

1 JOHN 4:19-21

Wherever we do not live communion among ourselves, communion with God is not alive and true.

Christians have always sought the smile of our Lady, this smile which medieval artists were able to represent with such marvelous skill and to show to advantage. This smile of Mary is for all; but it is directed quite particularly to those who suffer, so that they can find comfort and solace therein. To seek Mary's smile is not an act of devotional or outmoded sentimentality, but rather the proper expression of the living and profoundly human relationship which binds us to her whom Christ gave us as our Mother....

This smile, a true reflection of God's tenderness, is the source of invincible hope.

— *Homily at Mass for the Sick, Lourdes, France* (September 15, 2008)

THINK ABOUT IT

- Do I define my relationship with Mary by her loving smile?
- Do I seek the help and intercession of the Blessed Mother in my spiritual journey?
- Do I reflect on Mary's loving response to God's call? Do I practice her "yes" in my own life?

And Mary said,

"My soul magnifies the Lord,
and my spirit rejoices in God my Savior,
for he has regarded the low estate of his
handmaiden.
For behold, henceforth all generations will
call me blessed;
for he who is mighty has done great things
for me,
and holy is his name."

LUKE 1:46-49

REMEMBER

Hail Mary, full of grace. The Lord is with you. Blessed are you among women, and blessed is the fruit of your womb, Jesus.

We have just prayed the Rosary. Through these sequences of meditations, the divine Comforter seeks to initiate us in the knowledge of Christ that issues forth from the clear source of the Gospel text. For her part, the Church of the third millennium proposes to offer Christians the capacity for knowledge — according to the words of St. Paul — of God's mystery, of Christ, in whom are hid all the treasures of wisdom and knowledge (Col 2:2-3). Mary Most Holy, the pure and immaculate Virgin, is for us a school of faith destined to guide us and give us strength on the path that leads us to the Creator of Heaven and Earth. The Pope has come to Aparecida with great joy so as to say to you first of all, "Remain in the school of Mary." Take inspiration from her teachings; seek to welcome and to preserve in your hearts the enlightenment that she, by divine mandate, sends you from on high.

— *Address at the Basilica Shrine of Aparecida, Brazil* (May 12, 2007)

THINK ABOUT IT

■ The Rosary helps us to meditate on the mysteries of Christ's life and grow in our love for the Lord.

- Mary's intercession leads us to the heart of her Son, Jesus.
- Among the forms of popular devotion, the Rosary holds a unique position because of its relationship to the life of Christ and the faith of the Blessed Virgin Mary.

JUST IMAGINE

And he came to her and said, "Hail, full of grace, the Lord is with you!" But she was greatly troubled at the saying, and considered in her mind what sort of greeting this might be. And the angel said to her, "Do not be afraid, Mary, for you have found favor with God. And behold, you will conceive in your womb and bear a son, and you shall call his name Jesus.

> He will be great, and will be called the Son
>   of the Most High;
> and the Lord God will give to him the
>   throne of his father David,
> and he will reign over the house of Jacob
>   forever;
> and of his kingdom there will be no end."

LUKE 1:28-33

REMEMBER

The gentle, prayerful repetition of the prayers of the Rosary helps us to enter the silence of our hearts, where Christ's Spirit dwells.

MIKE AQUILINA, executive vice-president of the St. Paul Center for Biblical Theology, has authored or edited more than twenty books on Catholic history, doctrine, and devotion, including the best-selling *What Catholics Believe.* He is currently co-host of EWTN's *Reasons to Believe* and a regular panelist on *The Weekly Roman Observer* broadcast by the Catholic Family Network.

FATHER KRIS D. STUBNA received his doctorate in theology from the Pontifical Gregorian University in Rome. He is the diocesan secretary for education for the Diocese of Pittsburgh. Father Stubna is the author or co-author of several books, including *A Pocket Catechism for Kids.*

2 39 – 2 38 –
1346